TOPICS TODAY

The Fight Against Hate Crimes

By C. R. McKay

Cavendish Square
New York

Published in 2022 by Cavendish Square Publishing, LLC
29 E. 21st Street New York, NY 10010

First Edition

Website: cavendishsq.com

Portions of this work were originally authored by Michael V. Uschan and published as *Hate Crimes* (*Hot Topics*). All new material this edition authored by C. R. McKay.

All websites were available and accurate when this book was sent to press.

Cataloging-in-Publication Data

Names: McKay, C.R.
Title: The fight against hate crimes / C.R. McKay.
Description: New York : Cavendish Square, 2022. | Series: Topics Today | Includes index.
Identifiers: ISBN 9781502660985 (pbk.) | ISBN 9781502660992 (library bound) | ISBN 9781502661005 (ebook)
Subjects: LCSH: Hate crimes–Juvenile literature.
Classification: LCC HV6773.5 M35 2022 | DDC 364.15–dc23

Editor: Caitie McAneney
Copyeditor: Nicole Horning
Designer: Deanna Paternostro

CPSIA compliance information: Batch #CS22CSQ: For further information contact Cavendish Square Publishing LLC, New York, New York, at 1-877-980-4450.

Printed in the United States of America

CONTENTS

Introduction 5
"The Root of Evil Everywhere"

Chapter One 11
The Origins of Hate

Chapter Two 21
Race-Related Hate

Chapter Three 35
Attacks Based on Religion

Chapter Four 47
Anti-LGBTQ+ Hate Crimes

Chapter Five 55
Targeting Differences and Disabilities

Chapter Six 63
Who Commits Hate Crimes?

Chapter Seven 79
Driving Out Darkness

Getting Involved 89

Notes 90

For More Information 96

Index 100

Photo Credits 103

About the Author 104

COMMUNITY EMERGENCY HUB
Salaam
always be remembered
matter what..
love & Kindness will
RIP

"THE ROOT OF EVIL EVERYWHERE"

Violence based on bias against a person for their race, religion, sexual orientation, gender identity, or other differences is more than just a crime—it is a hate crime. No two hate crimes are alike. While some involve vandalism, arson, assault, or hate speech, others end in violent murders. Though they are all different, they are motivated by a hateful bias. Elie Wiesel, a Jewish survivor of a Nazi concentration camp during the Holocaust, said, "Hatred is at the root of evil everywhere. Racial hatred, ethnic hatred, political hatred, religious hatred. In its name, all seems permitted."[1]

Hate crimes are woven into the history of the United States, from the first European settlers to incite violence against Native peoples to enslavers to today's criminals who attack people for their immigrant status, skin color, or gender identity. Learning about the origins of hate and stereotyping, as well as the kinds of hate crimes that exist and who might be targeted, can lead to greater understanding and organizing for social justice in the United States and around the world.

Hate crimes leave a large impact on specific communities and the world as a whole. People left flowers to remember victims of a fatal anti-Muslim hate crime in Christchurch, New Zealand, in 2019.

What Counts as a Hate Crime?

The U.S. Department of Justice provides an easy equation for deciding if something is a hate crime:

A Crime + Motivation for Committing the Crime Based on Bias = Hate Crime

It seems like a simple black-and-white distinction. However, it is actually a very complex issue with many shades of gray. For one thing, "hate" is understood in this context not to mean anger or rage. Instead, it means a bias against people or groups with certain characteristics that are defined by law. Federal law and state laws sometimes differ on their definition of hate crimes. However, at the federal level, a crime is considered a hate crime if it is carried out based on a "victim's perceived or actual race, color, religion, national origin, sexual orientation, gender, gender identity, or disability."[2]

The crime itself is generally violent or destructive, such as arson, vandalism, assault, or murder. Threats to commit such crimes are also sometimes considered hate crimes. Hate crimes often affect far more than the individual who is harmed; they also affect people who share characteristics with that person. For example, if someone burns an individual's LGBTQ+ Pride flag, it is also hurtful to others in the LGBTQ+ community. Hate crimes can upset a community, a city, and even a whole nation.

People began to use the term "hate crime" to refer to offenses such as these in the late 1980s following the death of 23-year-old Michael Griffith, a Black man. Griffith was walking through Howard Beach, New York, on December 20, 1986, when three white people attacked him because they did not want Black people in their neighborhood. After beating Griffith, the white people chased him. Griffith was so terrified and wanted to get away from his tormentors so badly that he ran onto a busy highway. He died when a car struck him.

Griffith's death and other hate-related incidents created a growing awareness about this problem and led the U.S. Congress to pass the Hate Crime Statistics Act in April 1990. Annually since 1992, the Federal Bureau of Investigation (FBI) has collected and published data on hate crimes to keep law enforcement officials and the public aware of the problem. The FBI compiles the statistics with the help of state and local law enforcement officials. These statistics provide a rough idea of how many hate crimes take place in a given year, but they are not perfect. It can be hard to prove that bias was the main motive in some cases, even when a horribly violent act has occurred. The Marshall Project, which is a nonprofit group dedicated to journalism about criminal justice, says there is a problem with hate crime reporting by different jurisdictions. A 2019 analysis by the Marshall Project claimed, "For years, the number of hate crimes in the FBI's annual report has been consistently lower than that in the victim surveys ... Even when people choose to report hate crimes, what they believe to be an act of hate may not meet the legal standard."[3]

According to the Associated Press, not all state and local law enforcement agencies report hate crimes to the FBI. This means the numbers are likely much larger in reality. Experts say the FBI's numbers are not entirely reliable, but they are the best estimate the United States currently has. The Southern Poverty Law Center (SPLC) began tracking hate-crime reports after the 2016 presidential election. The SPLC titled their spring 2019 magazine issue "The Year in Hate: Rage Against Change." In the magazine issue, the SPLC painted a picture of an America in which hate groups, anti-Semitism, anti-immigrant stances, and hate crimes were on the rise. Hate groups, especially white supremacist groups, increased sharply after the 2016 presidential election of Donald Trump. In addition, anti-Semitic attacks, such as the Tree of Life synagogue shooting in Pittsburgh, Pennsylvania, in October 2018, rocked the country. The SPLC attributed some of the hate crimes and hate speech as stemming from fears over white people losing power and immigrants invading the county, as well as frustrations that Trump had not done enough. They also likely stemmed from a rage against change in the United States. The SPLC report claimed, "These fears and frustrations, heightened by

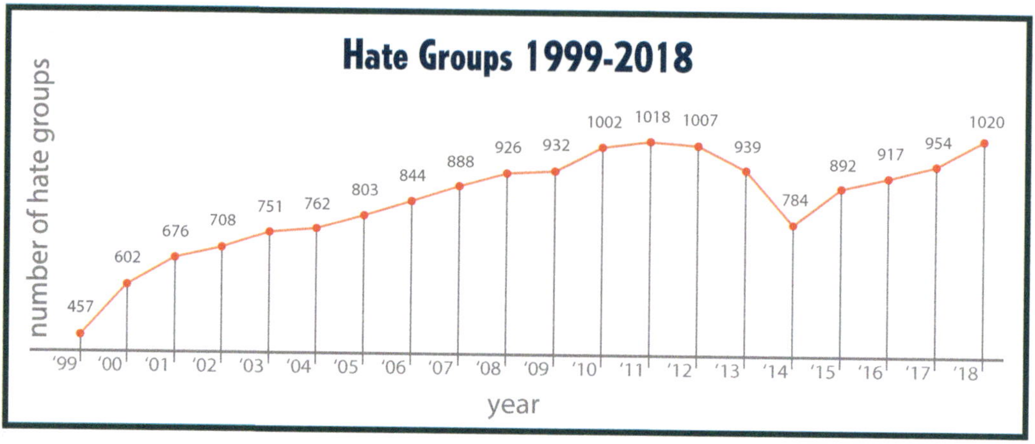

This chart from the Southern Poverty Law Center shows how the number of hate groups has changed from 1999 to 2018.

U.S. Census Bureau projections that white people will no longer be a majority by 2044, helped propel hate to a new high last year."[4] Research by organizations such as the SPLC and law enforcement agencies is critical in tracking the patterns of hate crimes, and how they are changing the social and political landscape of the country.

Yesterday, Today, and Tomorrow

You are probably familiar with at least one famous hate crime in history. During World War II, Nazis systematically murdered millions of people in what's come to be known as the Holocaust. The Nazis built death camps in which they killed many types of people whom they considered inferior because they were different: Jews, the Romani people, Slavic people from Poland and Russia, people who were gay or lesbian, and people with mental or physical disabilities. Throughout history, there have been many genocides across the world against people who are different. Genocide is the deliberate killing of a large group of people from a certain nation or ethnic group to try to wipe out this group of people completely. Some genocides are even happening today.

By understanding the hate crimes of previous generations, and tapping into the reasons behind hate, you can better understand the hate crimes of today and, hopefully, prevent more in the future. As civil rights activist W. E. B. Du Bois said, "Eastward and westward storms are breaking—great, ugly whirlwinds of hatred and blood and cruelty. I will not believe them inevitable."[5]

EMANUEL A.M.E. CHURCH

CHAPTER ONE

THE ORIGINS OF HATE

In 2017, a Georgia couple was sentenced to prison for their role in terrorizing an eight-year-old's birthday party. As part of a white supremacist group called "Respect the Flag," the pair waved Confederate flags, shouted racial slurs, and made armed threats against minorities there. What would motivate this couple to harm people they did not know, who had done nothing to them?

Many people feel hate in their lifetime, especially if they are hurt by someone else. This intense, passionate dislike for someone might cause someone to ignore or fight with that person. However, this emotion can also be directed at someone who has done nothing to the person. Sometimes it can become so intense that it causes unprovoked violence against others who are different.

Hate groups and online hate communities use this common human emotion of hate and fear to recruit people to their ranks. On June 17, 2015, 21-year-old Dylann Roof shot and killed nine Black Americans who were attending a Bible study at a church in Charleston, South Carolina. In the investigation of this mass murder, much about Roof's motivations was revealed. He claimed that he wanted to start a race war. Before committing this terrible crime, he spent a lot of time participating in white supremacist communities online and writing extensively about his belief that white people were being unfairly victimized by Black people. He thought the racist groups he found online were the only ones telling the real truth.

Shown here is Emanuel African Methodist Episcopal Church in Charleston, South Carolina, where Dylann Roof murdered nine people in an act of hate.

On these message boards, he found someone to blame for the difficulties he was experiencing in his life, and he found a community that supported his growing hatred. The prosecutor at his trial said that he had radicalized himself by seeking out hateful communities online and finding their biased views to be justification for his future violent plans. In 2016, a federal court convicted Roof of using a firearm to commit murder, and he was also convicted of civil rights violations, including hate-crime charges. He was sentenced to death.

To understand hate crimes like the one committed by Dylann Roof, it is important to look at the psychology behind hate, which in some circumstances, can lead to violent actions.

Finding the Familiar

Imagine you are getting on a school bus. It is your first day at a new school, and you do not know anyone. Who do you choose to sit next to? Odds are, you'll find someone who is like you in some way.

When humans see or meet other people for the first time, they note facts about them such as their age, their race, how they dress, and how they speak. Scientists have found that on a bus, people prefer to sit next to someone they know rather than a stranger. If they do not know anyone, they will generally look to share a seat with someone who is like them in some way—young or old, white or Black, male or female. People prefer to sit next to someone who shares a familiar characteristic with them because it makes that person seem less like a stranger. Sociologists and psychologists claim that most people are cautious about strangers due to a fear that goes back to humankind's primitive ancestors. Moving toward the familiar and away from the unfamiliar is a basic human instinct.

The 2004 book *Why We Hate* by Drs. Gordana Rabrenovic and Jack Levin explains that thousands of years ago, primitive people feared anyone who was not a member of their immediate group, whether that unit was a family or a tribe: "The survival of early humankind depended in part on being wary of strangers. Until and unless they were proven otherwise, outsiders were considered the enemy."[1] Fear helped people survive and decreased risks of attack. Levin and Rabrenovic argued that most humans today still instinctively fear people who are different or from a different group.

The differences humans use to assign other people to such groups are almost limitless. They range from race and religion to the school the other person attends and even the sports team they like. In her article "Understanding Hate," cultural psychologist Dr. Marianna Pogosyan wrote about key findings from psychologist Agneta Fischer's research:

> *Hate spreads and increases quicker if it's directed at a group, rather than an individual. When you hate a group, the intensity of your hate can grow without you being confronted with specific persons or contrasting information from the group—you are basing your hate on stereotypes and prejudices. If you hate an individual, your hate may be countered with empathy or a reappraisal of the person when you encounter their positive side.*[2]

This grouping of people causes people to think in "us vs. them" terms.

Us versus Them

Have you ever seen someone who dressed completely different from you and put them in a group? Someone who wears only sports jerseys might be seen as a "jock," and from there, you might assume many different things about them based on their inclusion in that group.

Dividing the world into "us" and "them" is a natural human instinct. Some psychologists call these groups the "in-group" (people who share similar qualities) and "out-group" (people who don't share the same qualities). However, when humans divide their world into "us" and "them," they no longer recognize members of out-groups as individuals; they see them only as units of a group. This is important because humans have different methods of relating to people they have assigned to a group and people they meet and judge on an individual basis.

Stereotypes are prejudgments of entire groups of people. Psychologists Robert M. Baird and Stuart E. Rosenbaum wrote the 1999 book *Hatred, Bigotry, and Prejudice: Definitions, Causes, & Solutions*. They claimed that humans generally rely on stereotypes to guide their actions toward people they consider different. Baird and Rosenbaum stated that people like to apply stereotypes about groups to all their members because it's faster and easier than assessing each person on an individual basis: "We humans have a need to simplify our interactions with others

The United States is a multicultural nation, becoming more diverse each year. More representation in government, media, and books can help people see past the "us vs. them" narrative.

into efficient patterns. This essential simplification leads naturally to stereotyping as a means to the desired efficiency."[3]

It makes sense, in this case, to categorize people into groups. However, this can lead to many issues, as each member of any group is an individual and has their own specific strengths and weaknesses. Also, stereotypes are often based on limited contact with a certain group of people, so they are often false. For example, Christians may have little contact with Muslims, white people may have little contact with Black people, and able-bodied people may have little experience with people who have disabilities. This makes it easy to make a false assumption about a group and to think of that group as a whole and not as individuals.

That leads to another problem with stereotypes—group stereotypes are almost always negative. A 2016 study by researchers at University College London found that the brain responds more strongly to information about groups who are portrayed negatively. The negative stories about a certain group add up over time, causing a strong prejudice to develop in a person's mind. Lead researcher Hugo Spiers claimed, "The negative groups become treated as more and more negative."[4] If faced with a story of someone from the negative group doing something positive, it was seen as unusual and did not break the prejudice toward the group as a whole.

Gordon W. Allport, a pioneer in the psychology of hatred, claimed that people willingly accept such negative stereotypes because of a basic human need to feel superior to others. Allport wrote, "The easiest idea to sell anyone is that he is better than someone else."[5] People are eager to

Animal Connections

Humans are not the only species to reject members who are different from them. A close primate relative, the chimpanzee, also shows aggressive behaviors toward "strangers." Those who study chimpanzees have found that unfamiliar chimps cause outrage, and are regularly attacked and killed. Author Sara Bullard wrote in her book *Teaching Tolerance*, "The insistence on the dominance of 'our' group and the antagonism toward strangers is very common among animals."[1] Bullard cited an observation by chimpanzee expert Jane Goodall. In 1966, Goodall observed a group of chimpanzees who had suffered from polio, which left some of them partially paralyzed, or unable to move certain body parts. Goodall watched as the other chimps showed fear toward the disabled chimps, threatening and attacking those who were different from the norm. How else do chimpanzees target the "other"? In 2018, a team of researchers from Leipzig University and the Max Planck Institute for Evolutionary Anthropology published a study looking at how chimpanzees decide who is "in" and who is "out" of their group. They found that chimps smell the difference in the urine of others. The lead author from this 2018 study, Stefanie Henkel, said, "Chimpanzees are highly territorial, and encounters between groups are mostly hostile—in fact, they sometimes kill individuals from other communities—so olfactory cues might help them to locate other animals and determine whether they are group members or strangers, enhancing their survival and leading to fitness benefits."[2]

1. Sara Bullard, *Teaching Tolerance: Raising Open-Minded, Empathetic Children* (New York, NY: Doubleday, 1996), p. 28.

2. Stefanie Henkel and Joanna Setchell, "Chimpanzees Sniff Out Strangers and Family Members," MAX-PLANCK-GESELLSCHAFT, October 24, 2018, www.mpg.de/12379440/1022-evan-019609-chimpanzees-sniff-out-strangers-and-family-members.

believe that their country, their race, their sports team, or their religion are better than others. This can lead to prejudice, or a preconceived negative attitude toward members of a particular group that's not based on facts.

Learning Hate

Some people think that kids are a "blank slate" when it comes to meeting new people. However, studies have found that by six months of age, babies can categorize people by gender and race. Numerous studies confirmed that by three to five years old, kids may start expressing bias based on race when interacting with other kids.

However, people are not born with prejudice. These stereotypes and prejudices are learned. In their 2002 book *Hate Crimes Revisited*, sociologists Jack Levin and Jack McDevitt discussed how people learn to hate others. They wrote, “Learning to hate is almost as inescapable as breathing … early on, merely by conversing with his family, friends, and teachers or by watching his favorite television programs, [a child] learns the characteristics of disparaging stereotypes.”[6]

One of the strongest influences in learned bias comes from cultural attitudes held by the people in the community, state, and region in which someone lives. Children learn from comments they hear daily from friends, neighbors, and other people. If people whom children respect make negative statements about Black, indigenous, people of color (BIPOC); LGBTQ+ people; or immigrants, or if they treat those people with disrespect, children will tend to adopt similar attitudes toward these groups. This is especially true if the person making the negative comment is an authority figure such as a teacher, a church leader, or an elected official.

A person’s family is another powerful influence. From the day children are born, parents and other relatives teach them a multitude of lessons about values, priorities, and attitudes. One of the most important lessons children learn from their parents is how to act toward other people. For example, if a child’s parents hate people of a certain race, they are likely to adopt similar racist feelings.

Media also shapes the social attitudes of young people. For example, if kids are exposed to racism and sexism in movies—even in cartoons—they may internalize that bias. Television shows and films sometimes lend believability to stereotypes by using them to shape how fictional characters are portrayed. Internet articles and news reports about minority communities influence how people feel about them, especially if the person watching or reading has not had much experience with that community. For example, news articles about high crime levels in Black neighborhoods may make readers feel that all Black people are criminals, even though that is not true.

Stereotypes, slurs, and prejudice are also woven into some popular music. Homophobic (antigay) slurs were used in Eminem’s rap

Some people deal with discrimination and hate speech based on their race even in school, which is supposed to be a safe space.

lyrics as recently as 2018. Racist and misogynistic (anti-women) slurs also find their way into popular tracks. Although some artists have been publicly criticized for prejudicial comments and lyrics, their popularity is hardly diminished by such controversy. They have huge fan bases, so the stereotypes they spread reach listeners around the world, influencing the beliefs of devoted fans. Some lyrics are even considered hate speech.

People are more likely to harm someone else if they think it is culturally acceptable. On October 6, 1998, college student Matthew Shepard was brutally murdered by Russell Henderson and Aaron McKinney for being gay. After meeting Shepard in a bar in Laramie, Wyoming, they robbed Shepard and beat him. They tied Shepard to a fence and left him to die; several days later, he died in the hospital from these wounds. Gregory M. Herek, a professor of psychology at the University of California, Davis, believes a major factor in this murder was that so many people in Wyoming hated gay people that this hatred was culturally acceptable. Herek claimed the two men thought their actions were justified by antigay sentiments they had heard throughout their lives. He wrote, "The killers most certainly had a lifelong exposure to society's messages about how men and women should behave and how homosexuals should be regarded. They may have believed that no one would mind the loss of another homosexual."[7]

Dehumanizing Humans

How can people who commit hate crimes justify their actions? The key is the dehumanization of the "other." Levin and McDevitt claimed that most people who commit hate crimes have something in common: a belief that their victims are so inferior to them that they cannot be considered human beings. This belief makes perpetrators feel it is all right

Hate Speech Hurts

Though you may have never witnessed a physically violent crime, most people are familiar with hate speech. Common slurs are used against LGBTQ+ individuals, people of different races, and people with disabilities. It might seem that the old saying is true: "Sticks and stones can break my bones, but words will never hurt me." However, hate speech has the ability to hurt, to threaten, and even to spark acts of violence.

The term "hate speech" refers to any form of expression designed to hurt or belittle members of a particular group. It includes offensive comments printed on pamphlets or posters, graffiti in the form of racist slogans or symbols painted on buildings, and symbolic acts such as burning a cross—a traditional tactic used by a hate group called the Ku Klux Klan (KKK) to frighten Black people and Catholics. Most hate speech is legal in the United States because the First Amendment to the U.S. Constitution guarantees freedom of speech.

However, hate speech is not harmless; it can encourage people to commit hate crimes. Donald Trump was elected president in 2016, after using hate speech against Latinx and Muslim people during his campaign. After his election, the number of reported hate crimes against Latinx and Muslim Americans increased, as some of Trump's supporters took his election as permission to openly express racist views. After Trump called Black Lives Matter protesters "terrorists" and "thugs," some of his supporters engaged in violent counter-protests. Michael Waltman, an associate professor at the University of North Carolina-Chapel Hill, said during the 2020 presidential race, "There's been a fairly long history, since he [Trump] got back into the election, of him basically using hate speech to promote his ideas. His immigration policy is grounded largely in xenophobia [fear of immigrants]."[1] This hate speech has spilled into white supremacist social media engagement, and between 2015 and 2017, the SPLC found that the number of likes and comments on hate group accounts grew by 900 percent. According to an FBI report, in 2018, hate crimes reached a 16-year high, especially against Latinx Americans.

1. Quoted in Nicquel Terry Ellis, "'Stand Back and Stand By': Rhetoric Some Call Racist has Marked Trump's Entire Presidency," *USA Today*, October 13, 2020, www.usatoday.com/story/news/politics/elections/2020/10/13/hate-speech-common-theme-trumps-presidency/5873238002/.

Shown here is a memorial for Matthew Shepard, who was brutally murdered for his sexual orientation.

to do things to their victims they would never think about doing to someone they considered human, including beating and even murdering them.

Dehumanizing the "other" is possible when people have had limited personal experience with that group, and it is much easier when they can harm a person or group indirectly. In the age of the internet, this is all too easy. The internet makes it possible to incite hatred and spread disinformation against a certain group, harass people without a physical confrontation, and connect people to hate groups.

Unfortunately, online harassment is difficult to stop. People can target others anywhere in the world, which means it is not always clear which police force has jurisdiction. Some of these people are skilled at hiding their location, so law enforcement agencies may not even be able to find them.

Many online hate crimes involve threats against women. In 2015, the *Telegraph* reported that "many women in public life have pointed out the online abuse they receive is not directed at what they have said or done, but at their gender. Sprinkled in amongst the general abuse and bomb threats has been a recurring motif: misogynistic and sexualized language and—almost invariably—threats of rape."[8] The layer of anonymity the internet provides makes it easy for people to dehumanize others and became an internet troll—and get away with it.

Your Opinion Matters!

1. Why might people be afraid to report a hate crime, and how could law enforcement agencies make it easier to do so?
2. Hate speech occurs both in person and online. How do you think people can shut down hate speech when they hear it?
3. How do you think people might be able to humanize the "other" in a situation where two people or two groups are at odds?

BLACK
LIVES
MATTER

RACE-RELATED HATE

In 2013, George Zimmerman was acquitted (found not guilty) for the killing of 17-year old Black high school student Trayvon Martin. In response to this acquittal, for an act which many people thought was a race-related hate crime, the Black Lives Matter movement began. Their website claims, "Black Lives Matter is an ideological and political intervention in a world where Black lives are systematically and intentionally targeted for demise. It is an affirmation of Black folks' humanity, our contributions to this society, and our resilience in the face of deadly oppression."[1]

Black Lives Matter has amplified Black voices around the topic of race-related hate, especially after the brutal May 2020 killing of George Floyd by a white policeman. Mostly peaceful protests and demonstrations erupted around the nation, calling for police reform and justice for Black Americans. However, the protests and Black Lives Matter demonstrations also led to a rise in hate crimes and violence against Black Americans.

In June 2020, an Illinois man was charged with a hate crime after running into Black Lives Matter protesters with his motorcycle. That same month, a white man in Wisconsin burned a biracial protester by throwing lighter fluid and a lighter at her, after shouting a racial slur. In July 2020, a white woman pointed a gun at a Black family in a restaurant parking lot. In several situations, white supremacists terrorized Black people around the country by leaving nooses as a threat.

Black Lives Matter marches and gatherings took place throughout the summer of 2020, even amid the COVID-19 pandemic.

Not every racially motivated hate crime is related to white supremacy, although some are. People may hold racist views without believing that all white people are inherently superior to people of color, and crimes motivated by racial bias can be carried out by people of all races, not just white people. Whenever a person is targeted for a crime because of their race, a hate crime has occurred. The United States has a long history with race-related hate crimes, going back to its very beginning.

Research on Racial Bias

In *Hate Crime Statistics 2019*, the FBI reported that 55.8 percent of all single-bias hate crimes were motivated by a bias of race, ethnicity, or ancestry. Of those 4,784 incidents, 48.4 percent were committed against Black people, 15.8 percent against white people, 14.1 percent against Latinx people, 4.3 percent against Asians, and 2.6 percent against American Indians or Alaskan Natives.

Statistics alone, though, fail to convey the human toll of hate crimes. In 2020, many hate crimes targeted Black Americans as the Black Lives Matter movement made large strides toward public awareness and change. In Warren, Michigan, a 24-year-old white man named Michael Frederick Jr. was arrested for terrorizing a Black family, the Halls, who had a Black Lives Matter sign in their window. The man fired shots into their house, threw a rock through their window, slashed their car tires, and wrote hurtful words on their pickup truck. This wasn't just one incident; the man committed the crimes across three separate nighttime sprees in early September 2020. The family could not sleep at night, living in fear of the next attack, until the suspect was arrested. Candace Hall, a victim of the attacks, said, "Hate brings no good to anyone."[2]

This attack, like many others each year, was motivated by a particular form of hatred—racism. In his book *White Supremacy*, George Frederickson explained that for some people, the physical, cultural, and social differences they have learned to hate can be attributed to a person's race: "Racists make the claim that such differences are due mainly to immutable [unchangeable] genetic factors."[3] Unfortunately, an increase in racist rhetoric and the organization of hate groups in the past few years has sparked many racist attacks.

A History of Hate Against Black Americans

Hate crimes against Black Americans are nothing new. Black Americans have faced extreme injustices in America since 1619, the year the first Black enslaved people were brought to the Virginia colony. For the next two centuries, Black people were bought and sold as property. They had no rights and were whipped for minor offenses such as talking back to their white enslavers—brutal treatment that today would be considered a hate crime.

Slavery ended in the United States with the passage of the 13th Amendment to the U.S. Constitution in 1865. However, the abolition of this cruel practice did not end mistreatment of Black Americans. White racists immediately began a campaign of violence to keep Black Americans politically and socially powerless. Acting individually or in groups such as the Ku Klux Klan (KKK), white people beat, raped, and murdered Black people. These white supremacists sought to keep Black Americans afraid, so they'd accept unfair conditions in the United States. This included forcing Black Americans to endure segregation, which was a legal and social system that reduced Black people to second-class citizens by denying them civil rights and forcing them to use separate facilities. Segregation was legal until 1964.

Lynching was both a hate crime and a highly effective, brutal scare tactic. This term originally meant putting a criminal to death without due process of law, but after the American Civil War (1861–1865), it became synonymous with organized brutality against Black Americans. Between 1882 and 1968, white people killed at least 3,446 Black men, women, and children by hanging, shooting, burning, stabbing, and torturing them. The violence continued unrestricted until the 1960s, when federal, state, and local governments finally began protecting Black people. The violence, however, still continues today, with cases of police brutality and hate crimes.

Racial Violence Continues

Racist ideas and race-related violence unfortunately aren't a thing of the past. Hate crimes against Black Americans are still the most common race-based crimes in the United States. White supremacist groups distribute literature and operate websites that demean Black Americans, record racist songs, and burn crosses. One common hate crime against Black people is to paint racist graffiti on homes and buildings.

The Tulsa Massacre

Perhaps one of the worst large-scale hate crimes against Black Americans in the 20th century was the Tulsa Race Massacre. The massacre, which occurred over 24 hours on May 31 to June 1, 1921, killed as many as 300 people. Hundreds of people were injured, and it is estimated that 8,000 or more people were left homeless.

Before the massacre, the Greenwood neighborhood in Tulsa, Oklahoma, was home to around 10,000 people. It was a thriving Black neighborhood, which had a business district known as Black Wall Street. Greenwood residents enjoyed restaurants, hotels, theaters, and stores run by Black business owners. The neighborhood was separate from the white areas of Tulsa, which saw high crime rates and racially motivated violence.

Then, on May 30, 1921, Dick Rowland—a Black teenager—entered an elevator. There was one other person on that elevator, a young white woman named Sarah Page. She screamed, and Rowland ran. He was arrested the next morning. However, the incident did not stop there. Rumors about what might have happened started to spread in the white community of Tulsa, fueled by a story in the *Tulsa Tribune*. An angry white mob gathered at the courthouse to get Rowland, causing a group of 25 armed Black men to meet at the courthouse to help guard Rowland from the white mob.

The tensions escalated quickly, until there were around 75 armed Black men and 1,500 white men at the courthouse, ready for a fight.

Some racist attacks are not only hurtful and sometimes deadly, but inhumanly brutal too. On June 7, 1998, 49-year-old James Byrd Jr. was murdered in Jasper, Texas. Three white men chained Byrd to a pickup truck and dragged him for 3 miles (4.8 kilometers). Shawn Allen Berry, one of the perpetrators, confessed that they had attacked Byrd because he was a Black American. The attack on Byrd by Shawn Allen Berry, John William King, and Lawrence Russell Brewer was not motivated by an argument or disagreement between Byrd and the white men; it was not motivated by theft or any other typical reason for a crime. Berry and the other two men attacked Byrd simply because of their hatred for Black Americans. Byrd remained alive through most of the attack, and the brutal slaying was

The Black men retreated soon after the skirmish began. However, white Tulsans started attacking random Black people in public. On the morning of June 1, thousands of white Tulsans swarmed into Greenwood, burning and stealing from Black homes and businesses in an area as wide as 35 city blocks. Witnesses even said that firebombs were dropped on the town. Greenwood was on fire.

Shown here is rubble left behind after the Tulsa Race Massacre.

The National Guard arrived, putting out fires and imprisoning thousands of Black Tulsans at the local fairgrounds. Hours later, Rowland was set free, as the police said he had not committed the crime he was held for. However, the damage was done; Greenwood, the Black Wall Street of America, was ruined.

For years, few people talked about the Tulsa Race Massacre, and mentions of it were not included in history books or taught in schools. Though the original death toll was reported as 26, the complete toll from the massacre could be around 300. Details are still being investigated today.

considered one of the most vicious hate crimes that had occurred in decades. Former Texas prosecutor Guy James Gray said, "When you handle a case like that and get inside the mind of a real racist, a white supremacist racist, and you see how dangerous those people are to the fabric of our society, you just become more sensitive to racial issues."[4]

In Jackson, Mississippi, in June 2011, a group of white teenagers drove around, looking for Black people to target. They attacked a 48-year-old Black man named James Craig Anderson. The attackers shouted "white power" as they attacked Anderson, and when he tried to stand up, they ran him over with a pickup truck, killing him. Mississippi state senator Barbara Blackman said, "Each time something like that occurs, whether

Psychologists are studying how racial trauma can be passed down through generations, creating anxiety for young people.

it is in Mississippi or in any place across this country, if you are a student of history, if you have any kind of conscience, then those kinds of horrific things should make you feel very uncomfortable."[5]

The National Association for the Advancement of Colored People (NAACP) reports that only about 2 percent of total hate crimes are reported to the FBI, so we do not know how many racially based hate crimes there are in the United States against Black Americans. One issue that could lead to underreporting is that some Black victims of hate crimes may think authorities would not believe them unless they had clear proof. In February 2018, Geoffrey Preudhomme spent an hour in his dorm room at Radford University in Virginia, hiding after his roommate threatened to kill him and shouted a racial slur at him. Preudhomme filmed the incident, and said, "In today's America, you have to be ready to film and document it, it's not just with brutality but in order to change the system we have to expose all versions of racism."[6]

Violence Against Native Peoples

Before Europeans arrived in North America, Native peoples had thriving communities and cultural practices. In the 1500s, when Spanish, French, and English explorers arrived on the shores of the land that would become the United States, they found Natives who had been there for thousands of years. The languages, cultures, and physical characteristics of these Native Americans—who are sometimes called First Americans or American Indians—all seemed strange to white Europeans. Europeans considered Native American cultures and religions inferior to European ways. Over the next three centuries, westward expansion of the United States to the Pacific Ocean came at the expense of Native Americans. Disease and violence wiped out large populations of Native peoples.

White settlers and U.S. officials used their belief that they were superior to Native Americans to justify taking their homelands and confining them to reservations. They sometimes took Native children and forced them to assimilate to white ways. Native Americans were not granted citizenship until 1924, when Congress passed the Indian Citizenship Act. The legislation was sparked by the heroic way in which thousands of Native Americans had fought for their country during World War I.

The new law, however, did not wipe out racism against Native Americans. Although the United States is the traditional homeland of Native Americans, the group's minority status and perceived physical and cultural differences set it apart from mainstream America. During the 1980s, Chippewa groups used treaty rights they had won a century earlier to use nets to catch walleyes in northern Wisconsin lakes. White people were angry that they would not be able to catch as many fish in the same lakes and resorted to violence to try to stop the Native Americans. White people issued death threats to tribal leaders and staged protests in which they carried racist signs. Today, the violence continues, though it is rarely charged as a hate crime. In May 2017, Jimmy Smith-Kramer—a 20-year-old member of the Quinault Indian Nation in Washington—was run over by a man who had been yelling racial slurs, according to bystanders. That man was never charged with a hate crime, even if many people believed it was motivated by anti-Native bias. This kind of case is discouraging for Native Americans who have been targeted and do not think they would be believed if they reported it.

While they often are not charged as hate crimes, Native American women are murdered and sexually assaulted on reservations and nearby towns at much higher rates than women of other ethnicities. Many times, their attackers are white or another non-Native race. In fact, white and non-Native American people commit more than two-thirds of sexual

White Supremacist Groups Today

Some people may think that hate groups like the KKK are a thing of the past. However, the KKK still exists, and new hate groups form each year. In March 2020, the SPLC reported that white nationalist hate groups in the United States had increased 55 percent during Trump's presidency. The racist movement continued to be driven by fears over demographic changes. In 2019, there were 155 white nationalist hate groups in the United States. That does not include KKK groups, racist skinheads, neo-Confederate groups, or Christian Identity groups. Some groups are part of the alt-right, which came to prominence in 2015 and shows nostalgia for pre-civil rights era America. Other white nationalist groups include The Base, Patriot Front, and American Identity Movement. In August 2017, a "Unite the Right" rally took over Charlottesville, Virginia, to protest the removal of a Confederate statue. This large, violent protest drew far-right extremists from around 39 states, many belonging to hate groups. Counter-protesters arrived, angering the far-right extremists. One of them drove a car into a crowd of counter-protesters, killing a person and injuring nearly 20 others.

Many white supremacist groups gained a sense of power under Trump's presidency and would not accept his loss in the 2020 election. They joined other Trump supporters at a "Save America"

assaults against indigenous women, as found in a study by the University of Delaware and the University of North Carolina. Many crimes against Native American women are not reported or data is not officially collected. A 2010 Government Accountability Office report found that federal prosecutors declined more than two-thirds of sexual abuse cases sent by tribal law enforcement to federal offices. Lisa Brunner, co-director of Indigenous Women's Human Rights Collective, said, "Native American women are victims of violence far greater than any population in the country simply because of who we are as Native women, and what we represent, our tribal nations."[7]

Violence Against Asians

The mid-19th century saw tens of thousands of Chinese immigrants coming to the United States after gold was discovered in California. From the rally in Washington, D.C., on January 6, 2020, as Congress was certifying electoral votes for President-elect Joe Biden. Egged on by Trump's calls for them to march to the Capitol, this mob stormed the Capitol, put the lives of U.S. leaders at risk, and tried to overturn a fair election. Many carried Confederate flags and wore white nationalist symbols. Political writer Brandon Tensley linked the attack on the U.S. Capitol to "White backlash," writing, "White backlash to racial equality—including an empowered Black electorate—isn't unusual. In fact, what makes the dynamic disturbing is how common it's been throughout U.S. history."[1]

Alt-right protesters with torches surround counter-protesters by a statue of Thomas Jefferson in Charlottesville, Virginia, during the Unite the Right rally in 2017.

1. Brandon Tensley, "The US Capitol Attack Fits into the History of White Backlash," CNN, January 13, 2021, www.cnn.com/2021/01/13/politics/capitol-mob-white-backlash-history/index.html.

beginning of their immigration, they faced discrimination and violence, and hate crimes against Asian people still happen today. For many decades, Chinese men and women were denied citizenship and other rights and were forced to live in segregated areas in cities. Some white people physically attacked Chinese men and women, and large groups sometimes invaded Chinatowns to burn and destroy businesses and homes.

Succeeding waves of immigrants from other Asian countries have faced similar racial hatred since then. Southeast Asians from Vietnam, Laos, and Cambodia fled to the United States after the Vietnam War ended in 1975 because they did not want to live in a Communist country. On July 14, 2001, Thung Phetakoune, a 62-year-old immigrant from Laos, was murdered in Newmarket, New Hampshire. Richard Labbe said he shot Phetakoune because he was angry with the Asian Communists who

March 2020 was a tense time in America, as the COVID-19 virus—and racial violence against Asians—spread rapidly. Members of the Asian American Commission are shown here speaking out at the Massachusetts State House to condemn this racism.

had killed his relatives in combat and Phetakoune's outward appearance matched Labbe's stereotype of an Asian Communist.

The COVID-19 pandemic was traced back to Wuhan, China, in late 2019. The virus crashed economies, killed more than a million people in 2020, and turned the world upside down. As COVID-19 spread across the world, so did anti-Asian sentiments. The Anti-Defamation League (ADL) reported a surging increase in racist and xenophobic (anti-immigrant) attacks targeting members of the Asian American and Pacific Islander community in the United States. People blamed Asians for "bringing the virus," yelled racial slurs, and physically assaulted Asians. In one instance, in March 2020, two women attacked a Chinese American man while he was jogging. They told him to go back to China, threw a log at him, and spat on him.

Anti-Latinx Hate Crimes

While "Latinx" is not technically a race and Latinx people can be any race, it is often viewed similarly to a racial group in the United States. "Latinx" often refers to a person of Latin American descent. Latin America includes the countries of Central and South America. While England settled much of North America, Spain settled much of South and Central America. Their cultures mixed with indigenous cultures to create unique ways of life. The history of Latinx discrimination and injustice in the United States is long and often bloody.

As English settlers moved south and west across North America, border disputes and culture clashes occurred. The treaty that ended the Mexican-American War (1846–1848) led to the Mexican Cession, in which Mexico had to give up 55 percent of its territory. This included all or some of today's Arizona, California, New Mexico, Texas, Colorado, Nevada, and Utah. Many Mexican lands soon belonged to the United States, and people living there had a tough choice—move, or be incorporated into the United States. Because of this, and a long land border between Mexico and the United States, many Latinx individuals live in the United States today. In a 2019 interview with NPR, Monica Muñoz Martinez, author of *The Injustice Never Leaves You: Anti-Mexican Violence in Texas* and an assistant professor of American studies at Brown University, said there is "a history of forgotten lynchings of Mexican Americans and Mexican nationals," some even "at the hands of police, of U.S. soldiers, in some cases people who were collaborating with vigilantes."[8]

These anti-Latinx hate crimes are on the rise. The 2019 FBI report on hate crimes revealed 527 incidents against Latinx individuals, and the number of anti-Latinx hate crimes rose by more than 21 percent from 2017 to 2018. This coincides with an increase in anti-immigration rhetoric from politicians and the far-right, especially President Trump, who spoke against Mexicans during his 2016 presidential campaign and talked about a "caravan" of Latinx immigrants entering the United States in 2018. Part of his 2016 presidential campaign platform included promises to build a border wall across the U.S. border with Mexico to keep undocumented immigrants out. These speeches about an "invasion" of Latinx immigrants had real—and violent—consequences.

One of the most striking anti-Latinx hate crimes to stem from these speeches was the 2019 El Paso, Texas, shooting. Patrick Crusius, a 21-year-old white man, drove more than 11 hours to El Paso to kill Latinx people at a Walmart. He killed 22 people and injured 26 others. Before he started shooting, he posted to a white supremacist site about his racist, anti-immigrant beliefs, reportedly aiming to stop the "Hispanic invasion of Texas."

Shown here is a memorial for the 22 victims of the El Paso shooting outside the Walmart where it occurred in 2019.

Human Cost and Lives Lost

The statistics of race-based hate crimes can give you an idea of how many lives have been lost or how many people have been directly affected by hate crimes. However, it is hard to capture the true cost of hate crimes, as they affect not only the victim and their family, but also an entire race or community. Hate crimes not only harm the victim but also other people of the same race by frightening, humiliating, or intimidating them.

Cross burnings are an example of a hate crime that affects an entire racial group. In an opinion defending a Virginia law that outlaws cross burnings, U.S. Supreme Court justice Clarence Thomas, an African American, declared, "There is no other purpose to the [burning] cross—no communication, no particular message. It was intended to cause fear and to terrorize a population."[9] Such acts also divide communities by increasing tensions among all white and Black residents.

The greatest harm that hate crimes cause, however, is to victims and their families. When the Hall family was terrorized for multiple nights by white supremacist Michael Frederick Jr., the impact of the fear they felt stayed with them. Though Candace Hall said she forgave the suspect for his acts of hate, she also said that her teenage daughter was still troubled by the nighttime attacks.

Sometimes people who commit hate crimes regret their actions when they realize there are consequences, and that their actions affected real human beings and not just a stereotype in their head. Michael

Racial Retaliation

Sometimes people of color are on the other end of hate crimes. They may target other races out of retaliation for wrongs against their race, or try to protect their territory in a neighborhood. On October 7, 1989, in Kenosha, Wisconsin, a group of Black men watched *Mississippi Burning*, a film about white racists killing a Black civil rights worker. Afterward, they saw a 14-year-old white boy walking down the street. The Black men decided to take out their anger over what they had seen in the movie on the white boy. They beat him severely and stole his sneakers.

Black and Latinx people sometimes commit hate crimes against each other. In Los Angeles, California, members of a Latinx gang were charged with a hate crime for murdering Kenneth Wilson in 1999. Assistant U.S. attorney Alex Bustamante said they killed Wilson "because he was black [and] gang members had promised each other, had agreed that they would drive African Americans out of the neighborhood, by threats, by force, by murder."[1] Bustamante said the murder was part of a six-year gang effort to keep Black people from moving to their neighborhood. All four defendants were convicted. This is another example of the "us vs. them" mindset, even when it is not a dominant group targeting a minority group.

1. Quoted in John Spano, "Hate Crime Charged in Gang Killing," *Los Angeles Times*, June 29, 2006, p. B5.

Frederick Jr. ended up apologizing for terrorizing the Hall family. During his statement in court, he said, "I just want Mr. and Mrs. Hall … I want them to forgive me, judge … I'm extremely regretful of what I did."[10]

Your Opinion Matters!

1. Slavery and segregation are dark, violent parts of U.S. history. In what ways are we still seeing the effects of this violent ideology?
2. How might the COVID-19 pandemic cause an increase in hate crimes based on racial bias?
3. How might people break the cycle of hate in areas that are becoming increasingly diverse?

ATTACKS BASED ON RELIGION

The First Amendment to the U.S. Constitution—part of the Bill of Rights—provides citizens the freedom of religion. In fact, some of the first English settlers to come to what became the United States did so to escape religious persecution and have the ability to practice their faith without fear. In the 400 years since those settlers arrived, immigrants of all religions have come from around the world to make their home in the United States. Unfortunately, just because U.S. citizens have the right to practice their religion does not mean there are no religion-biased hate crimes. For many religious groups, the number of violent and threatening incidents are actually on the rise.

The 2019 FBI report on hate crimes found that of the single-bias hate crimes, 21.4 percent were based on religion. Of the 1,650 religion-biased hate crime incidents, 60.3 percent were motivated by anti-Jewish bias—making Jewish people the most targeted group. That year, 13.3 percent of religious-biased hate crimes were motivated by anti-Islamic (Muslim) bias, 4 percent were motivated by anti-Catholic bias, 3.6 percent were motivated by anti-Christian bias, and 3 percent were motivated by anti-Sikh bias. Smaller religious communities in the United States that have been targeted are Mormons, Hindus, Buddhists, and Eastern Orthodox Christians.

Nazi symbols, such as the salute and swastika shown here, are often used by groups that target Jewish communities and individuals today.

The Roots of Religious Hatred

Even though the main message in most religions is love and respect for fellow humans, there has been violence over religion for thousands of years. Members of the world's three major religions—Christianity, Judaism, and Islam—have, at times, hated and warred against each other because they believe their belief system is the only true one. Individual religions have also been divided over the proper way to worship the same God. Roman Catholicism and Protestantism are both Christian religions, but their members have often clashed because of differences in some of their beliefs and traditional ways of worship.

Followers of Jewish, Christian, and Muslim religions brought those ancient hatreds with them when they immigrated to the United States—a fact that is reflected in statistics on U.S. hate crimes motivated by religious bias. Some of these hateful incidents include vandalism and arson against places of worship, while other acts are deadly.

Hate for the Jewish Community

Anti-Semitism is prejudice against or hostility toward Jewish people. Jews have faced hatred and violence for thousands of years. When Christianity became the religion of the Romans, they destroyed the Jewish state and scattered Jews around the ancient world. As time went on, Jews were persecuted and discriminated against throughout Europe. They were denied civil and legal rights in many places, and even massacred. One of the worst acts of violence against Jews was the Holocaust. Adolf Hitler's Nazi regime started persecuting Jews in 1933, but between the years 1941 and 1945, he led a state-sponsored mass murder of Jews, LGBTQ+ individuals, people with disabilities, and ethnic minorities. Approximately 6 million Jews were killed in the Holocaust, many in concentration camps.

The Holocaust brought worldwide attention to the suffering of Jews in Europe. However, Jewish people have also faced hate in the United States, even after the Holocaust. Jewish people did not begin immigrating to the United States in large numbers until the late 19th century. Anti-Semitism grew stronger as the number of Jewish immigrants grew. This hatred resulted in employment and social

Nazis Then, Neo-Nazis Now

Nazis were members of the National Socialist German Workers' Party, which ruled Germany from 1933 to 1945. Their leader was Adolf Hitler, who capitalized on the economically depressed and politically unstable conditions in Germany after World War I. Hitler ran on a platform of German nationalism and anti-Semitism. He attracted new members to the Nazi Party through impassioned speeches that blamed Jews and other groups for the problems in Germany. He declared that Aryans were the master race and targeted Jews through laws that banned marriage between Jews and Christians and even banned Jews from most public places in Germany. He was very successful in painting a negative picture of "the other" and dehumanizing Jews. Nazis moved into other parts of Europe, killing Jews in Poland in mass numbers. In 1942, the Nazis began the last phase of the "Final Solution" to the "Jewish problem" with a strategy to murder all European Jews. European Jews from countries including Poland, France, Belgium, and Germany were taken to death camps and killed by the millions. When Germany lost World War II, the Allies occupied Germany and outlawed the Nazi Party.

The fall of the Nazi Party did not end Nazi influence. Today, neo-Nazis still use many of the ideas of the Nazis. They also use the same symbol—a swastika, which was part of the Nazi flag. The ADL reported that of the 919 anti-Semitic vandalism incidents in 2019, 746 involved swastikas. The Southern Poverty Law Center claims, "Neo-Nazi groups share a hatred for Jews and a love for Adolf Hitler and Nazi Germany. While they also hate other minorities, gays and lesbians and even sometimes Christians, they perceive 'the Jew' as their cardinal enemy."[1] There are neo-Nazi groups in Europe as well as in the United States.

1. "Neo-Nazi," Southern Poverty Law Center, last modified November 8, 2020. www.splcenter.org/fighting-hate/extremist-files/ideology/neo-nazi.

discrimination against Jews, who also became targets of violence that today would be considered hate crimes. Anti-Semites, including members of the KKK, beat up or murdered Jewish people and burned down synagogues.

Christians have committed most of the hate crimes against Jews. The traditional basis for Christian anti-Semitism is the belief that Jews were responsible for killing Jesus Christ, even though it was a Roman official who ordered his death and Roman soldiers who crucified him. Jews and Muslims have also clashed, as tensions between the Jewish nation of Israel and its surrounding Muslim countries spill over into Jewish and Muslim communities in the United States.

Hate crimes motivated by anti-Semitism make up the highest percentage of religion-based hate crimes in the United States. The year 2019 was especially troubling, as the American Jewish community experienced the highest level of anti-Semitic incidents since tracking began in 1979. The ADL found more than 2,100 acts of assault, vandalism, and harassment against Jewish people in that one year. Jonathan A. Greenblatt, CEO of the ADL, said, "This was a year of unprecedented [anti-Semitic] activity, a time when many Jewish communities across the country had direct encounters with hate … This contributed to a rising climate of anxiety and fear in our communities."[1]

On April 27, 2019, 19-year-old John Earnest opened fire on the Jewish synagogue Chabad of Poway in San Diego, California. He killed a woman named Lori Kaye, and injured three more people, including an 8-year-old girl, during a Passover service. Earnest had

Mourners pray in front of the Tree of Life Synagogue in Pittsburgh, Pennsylvania. In October 2018, a man armed with an assault rifle opened fire on a service there, killing 11 people and wounding others. He shouted anti-Semitic slurs as he attacked.

written a long letter about his disgust for Jews. He greatly admired other mass shooters, including a gunman who killed 11 people in a Pittsburgh, Pennsylvania, synagogue only months before. Greenblatt said, "This was a pointed attack on Chabad, on the visible Jewish community here, and this is a collective attack on all Jewish communities — this is anti-Semitism unleashed."[2]

Islamophobia in America

The second most-targeted religion in the United States is Islam. Followers of Islam are called Muslims. Many, but not all, Muslims can trace their roots back to Arab countries in the Middle East. Because of that, they are often mistaken for Arabs, and Arabs are often mistaken for Muslims. Political tensions between the United States and the Middle East have often incited hate crimes against Arabs and Muslims living in the United States, which was the case during the Persian Gulf War (1990–1991). Some people wrongly blamed Muslims and Arabs for the Oklahoma City Bombing in 1995 and the explosion of TWA Flight 800 in 1996. However, Islamophobia—the fear of and hate against Muslims—truly boomed after the terrorist attacks of September 11, 2001.

In the first month after the September 11 attacks, more than 300 hate crimes against Muslims occurred in 38 states. By the end of 2001, the number of such offenses had nearly tripled. People shouted slurs at Muslims; made telephoned death threats; vandalized and set fire to Muslim mosques, homes, and businesses; and beat up Muslims. In several incidents, American Muslims were even murdered. These incidents happened despite the fact that most American Muslims condemned the attacks, which had killed Muslims as well as members of other religions.

Thousands of mosques in the United States became the main targets of people who hated Muslims. During the first few years after the September 11 attacks, dozens of these places of worship were vandalized with graffiti or damaged by arson fires and bombs. In Florida, one man smashed his truck into the Islamic Center of Tallahassee. In April 2006, shots were fired into a Maryland mosque, and in June 2006, a sign that claimed "Muslims Worship Satan" was left near an Arizona mosque. Some people desecrated, or publicly ruined, the

Quran, which is the holy book of Islam. They burned the Quran or spit on it in public displays of hate.

Anti-Muslim feeling remained high in the United States because of the nation's continuing war against al-Qaeda and other Muslim terrorist groups, which included invasions of Afghanistan and Iraq. Combat deaths of U.S. soldiers in those two countries were a major source of Muslim hatred, even though many American Muslims also fought and died for their country during those wars.

During the 2016 presidential campaign season, hate crimes against Muslims rose again. The number of assaults against Muslims in the United States from 2015 to 2016 even surpassed those of 2001. The next year saw another 17 percent increase in anti-Muslim hate crimes. In a 2016 article for the *New York Times*, Eric Lichtblau wrote, "Some scholars believe that the violent backlash against American Muslims is driven not only by the string of terrorist attacks that began early last year, but also by the political vitriol from candidates like Donald J. Trump, who has called for a ban on immigration by Muslims and a national registry of Muslims in the United States."[3] Many people drew a

This man is shown holding up an anti-Muslim sign in Cleveland, Ohio, in July 2016, falsely claiming that all Muslims are "jihadists," or violent Islamist extremists.

connection between hateful speeches before the 2016 election and the rise in anti-Muslim assaults.

Attacks against Muslims happen all over the world. In March 2019, a 28-year-old Australian man killed 51 people and injured dozens more when he opened fire on two mosques in Christchurch, New Zealand. The gunman, Brenton Tarrant, was a white supremacist who officials described as a "right-wing extremist terrorist." Before he attacked, Tarrant posted a manifesto (a public declaration of motives) on social media describing his white nationalistic views and praising mass murderers such as Dylann Roof. Tarrant live-streamed his mass murder on social media. The killings shook the Muslim community.

Iman Atta is a director of Tell MAMA (Measuring Anti-Muslim Attacks), a national project which records and measures anti-Muslim incidents in the United Kingdom. She responded to an increase in anti-Muslim hate crimes after the Christchurch attacks, saying, "This shows that some people see Muslims as fair game for hate and it is now clear that we have an ongoing and persistent ideology of hate that is generating a focus on Muslims."[4]

Protesters in Melbourne, Australia, marched against racism and Islamophobia in 2019 in response to the Christchurch attacks.

Mistaken for Muslim

Some people have been targets of Muslim-bias hate crimes even if they are not Muslim. Mistaken identity has played a part in many hate crimes following the September 11 terrorist attacks. In seeking revenge on Muslim Arab terrorists, some perpetrators accidentally targeted non-Muslim Arab Americans as well as people from several countries who were neither Arab nor Muslim. On September 23, 2001, an arson fire at St. George's Assyrian Church in Chicago, Illinois, caused $250,000 in damage. Although the church's members are from Arab countries, they are Christians.

Sikhs are often mistaken for being Muslim. The Sikh religion, which started in South Asia in the 15th century, is a monotheistic faith that leans heavily toward equality and social justice. Because the men wear turbans for religious reasons, they are often targeted for being immigrants and mistaken for being Muslim. On September 15, 2001, Frank Roque shot and killed Balbir Singh Sodhi in Mesa, Arizona. Roque wanted to kill an Arab Muslim to get revenge for the September 11 attacks. Sodhi, however, was from India and was a member of the Sikh religion. Roque thought he was an Arab Muslim because he wore a turban and had a long beard, both of which are Sikh cultural traditions. These features made Sodhi look like Roque's stereotyped conception of Arab Muslims, who sometimes wear head coverings called kaffiyehs and often have beards. This was not an isolated incident. In 2003, several Sikh cab drivers in the San Francisco, California, area were shot to death.

Crimes Against Catholics

There are many different branches of Christianity. The United States is a mostly Christian nation, so these groups are not targeted as much as Jews and Muslims. However, one Christian group has been targeted by other Christians—Roman Catholics. American Catholics have faced religious discrimination and hate crimes since the 1600s, when they first began immigrating to the English colonies that would one day become the United States. Most anti-Catholic sentiment came from

In 2014, the Sikh Coalition published a report about bullying against Sikh children in schools. They found that more than two-thirds of Sikh students get bullied at school, and children who wear turbans experience bullying at more than double the rate of other children. Many were accused of being Islamic terrorists, even though they were not Muslim, and accused of hiding explosives in their head coverings. The 2014 report stated, "The period since 9/11 has been particularly difficult for Sikh Americans and their children. While Sikh children experience bullying in the classrooms, their Sikh American parents endure astoundingly high rates of hate crimes, employment discrimination, and scrutiny at the nation's airports. Brown skin and turbans have popularly become associated with terror."[1]

Sikh men are easily identified by their turbans. However, sometimes they are attacked because of it.

1. "Go Home Terrorist": *A Report on Bullying Against Sikh American School Children*. The Sikh Coalition, 2014, p. 4.

Protestants, who are members of a separate branch of Christianity who disagree with some Catholic beliefs and forms of worship. Protestants dominated the colonies, and at times, they barred Catholics from practicing their faith. When large numbers of Irish and other European Catholics began immigrating to the United States during the 19th century, Protestants used their economic and political power to discriminate against Catholics in jobs and housing. Protestant gangs attacked Catholics and their churches, sometimes destroying the churches.

John F. Kennedy was the first Catholic president of the United States. However, he was assassinated in 1963.

In 1960, John F. Kennedy overcame this prejudice to be elected the first Catholic U.S. president, and much of the discrimination over Catholicism eased. In recent years, some hate crimes aimed at the Catholic Church have been linked to outrage over decades of sexual misconduct by some priests.

The summer of 2020 saw a rise in anti-Catholic incidents. Catholic churches and statues were vandalized and burned across the country. In July 2020, 23-year-old Steven Shields was arrested after driving a minivan into the front door of Queen of Peace Catholic Church in Ocala, Florida. He threw gasoline on the foyer and set it on fire. That same month, a statue of Jesus was beheaded at Good Shepherd Church in Miami, Florida. Some of the offenders had issues with the history of the Catholic Church or with the religious figures depicted in statues.

Targeting Smaller Religious Communities

Smaller religions also face hate in the United States. Attacks based on anti-Hindu bias were on the rise from 2015 to 2019 when the FBI hate crimes report was released. In 2019, a Hindu priest was brutally attacked in Queens, New York, which some thought was a hate crime. That same year, a white teenager vandalized a Hindu temple in Louisville, Kentucky. Samir Kalra, managing director of the Hindu American Foundation, said:

> *The FBI stats, while helpful, do not represent a complete picture of the extent of hate crimes faced by Hindu Americans. Many incidents don't get reported by victims or are not recorded by law enforcement. Similarly, many bias incidents against Hindus may not be recorded under the anti-Hindu category due to mistaken identity. For instance, some incidents motivated by anti-Arab or anti-Muslim sentiment may actually involve Hindu victims. Moreover, some crimes*

Mt. Pleasant Baptist Church was one of several churches in Opelousas, Louisiana, to be burned during Easter week in 2019.

against Hindus may be based on their racial or ethnic identity and consequently be categorized under a racial/ethnic category instead.[5]

No other minority religion has been more targeted in recent years in the United States than Sikhs. The 2018 FBI hate crimes report showed a 200 percent increase in anti-Sikh hate crimes. In July 2020, a Denver, Colorado, man was charged with a hate crime for running over a Sikh man after reportedly telling him to "go back to your country." That same month, a Sikh temple in Orangevale, California, was vandalized with the words "white power" and a swastika.

Black Baptist churches are sometimes targets of vandalism and arson, though this generally has a racial bias. As with Sikhs and Hindus, it can be hard to separate religious and racial bias in some cases. One thing is true: Such hate crimes do more harm than merely damaging places of worship. They also create mental and emotional anguish for the members of that religion.

Your Opinion Matters!

1. How can religious communities help prevent violent religious extremism and hate crimes from happening?
2. How can you still see the effects of the 2001 terrorist attacks on Muslim life and Islamophobia in the United States?
3. In what ways can vandalism of places of worship harm a religious community?

POSE
6·11 FX
6·11 FX
6·11 FX
POSE

CHAPTER FOUR

ANTI-LGBTQ+ HATE CRIMES

After race and religion, the third most common single-bias hate crime type is based on sexual orientation. After that, it is violence based on gender identity bias. LGBTQ+ stands for lesbian, gay, bisexual, transgender, and queer or questioning, plus other sexual orientations and gender identities that do not fit the "norm" in society. People have been persecuted for their sexual orientation and gender identity for thousands of years, and on June 12, 2016, LGBTQ+ individuals were targeted in one of the deadliest mass shootings in U.S. history. Omar Mateen opened fire in Pulse nightclub, a well-known gay bar, in Orlando, Florida. He killed 49 people and seriously wounded dozens more.

Mateen's motives may have included racist and religious biases, and the Pulse nightclub shooting was classified as a hate crime against LGBTQ+ people. The shooter claimed to be a member of the militant Islamist terrorist organization ISIS, although he was not directly connected to the group in any way. Instead, it seems he learned their hateful ideology through the internet and carried out the attack on his own. He was killed after barricading himself in a bathroom during the attack.

Acceptance around different sexual orientations and gender identities has grown throughout the 21st century, especially as

Pose is a TV drama that stars many LGBTQ+ actors, including those shown here. *Refract Magazine* said, "Representation of queer and transgender people of color in 'Pose' is important because it presents them as normal people with normal problems, and allows for their further integration into society."[1]

Understanding Identity and Sexuality

A person's sexual orientation is the emotional, romantic, or sexual attraction they feel toward another person. People attracted to members of the opposite sex are often called "straight." People attracted to members of the same sex are called "gay" or "lesbian," depending on their gender. Bisexual people are attracted to both sexes. Gender identity does not explicitly involve sexual orientation, but transgender individuals are included in the LGBTQ+ community. Transgender people have a different gender identity than the sex they were assigned at birth. The Human Rights Campaign defines gender identity as "one's innermost concept of self as male, female, a blend of both or neither – how individuals perceive themselves and what they call themselves."[1] A person's gender expression is the external appearance of their gender identity, often expressed through clothing, haircut, or behavior.

Some people say that LGBTQ+ people are targeted because of their lifestyle. However, this makes it seem as if sexuality and gender identity are just lifestyle choices. In fact, they are a mix of biology, psychology, and environmental factors, and not simply something that can be chosen or "shut out." Some scientific studies have even shown that genes and hormones can play a role in a person's sexuality and identity. Transgender activist Jazz Jennings wrote, "Ever since I could form coherent thoughts, I knew I was a girl trapped inside a boy's body. There was never any confusion in my mind. The confusing part was why no one else could see what was wrong."[2]

Transgender people face discrimination and even brutal attacks for their gender identity.

1. "Sexual Orientation and Gender Identity Definitions," Human Rights Campaign, www.hrc.org/resources/sexual-orientation-and-gender-identity-terminology-and-definitions (accessed November 8, 2020).

2. Jazz Jennings, "When I First Knew I Was Transgender," *TIME*, May 31, 2016, time.com/4350574/jazz-jennings-transgender/.

media representation has increased. Even so, anti-LGBTQ+ violence is extremely common, and many members of this community are the victims of hate crimes each year. Because of who they are attracted to or how they identify themselves, LGBTQ+ individuals may be targets of hate crimes.

Behind the Numbers

Bias against sexual orientation made up 16.8 percent of the single-bias hate crimes in 2019, followed by 2.8 percent for gender-identity bias. The FBI reported 1,395 victims who were targeted for their sexual orientation. Antigay bias was most common at 62.2 percent of those victims, followed by a mixed-group bias (against all LGBTQ+ people) at 24.5 percent.

The 2019 FBI hate crimes report showed 227 victims of gender-identity bias. Of those victims, 175 were victims of anti-transgender bias. The transgender community unfortunately experiences some of the most brutal murders associated with any category of hate crimes. However, these sensational homicides are only a small percentage of the total number of offenses caused by hatred of a person's sexual orientation or gender identity. The National Coalition of Anti-Violence Programs (NCAVP) published a report on the state of anti-LGBTQ+ violence in 2017. The NCAVP stated:

> *Hate violence is a far too common and too often deadly experience for lesbian, gay, bisexual, transgender, queer (LGBTQ) and HIV-affected people. Hate violence is enacted in many different ways, including physical violence, verbal harassment, sexual violence, and discrimination, and is distinct from other forms of violence in that it targets people for their real or perceived identities.*[2]

Gregory M. Herek is an expert on sexual-orientation hate crimes. He believes federal statistics paint a flawed portrait of the frequency of such offenses because many victims never report them to officials. Herek wrote, "Estimates of nonreporting among gay and lesbian hate crime victims [in various studies] have ranged as high as 90 percent."[3] Herek said that many victims do not report crimes because they believe law enforcement officials will discriminate against or mistreat them—a fear that is based on past incidents in which this has sometimes happened. The violent history between police and LGBTQ+ people is evidenced by the 1969 Stonewall Riots. Police violently raided the Stonewall Inn, a Greenwich Village (New York City) gay club, sparking days of protest and the beginning of the modern gay rights movement. Many victims also fear that they will suffer negative consequences from employers, friends, or even spouses if their sexual orientation is publicly revealed in a criminal complaint.

Another reason why LGBTQ+ hate crimes are underreported is because law enforcement officials and the justice system often do not categorize them as such offenses. They may also overlap with race hate crimes or be labeled as a sexual assault and not a hate crime. The brutal 2002 slaying of Gwen Araujo in Newark, California, is an example of this. Araujo, a 17-year-old transgender woman, was kicked and beaten with an iron skillet, struck with a shovel, and choked with a rope. On September 12, 2005, a jury convicted two men of second-degree murder in Araujo's death but found them innocent of hate-crime charges. Thom Lynch, former executive director of the San Francisco Lesbian, Gay, Bisexual, and Transgender Community Center at the time of the verdict, criticized the jury's decision: "Only some justice has been done. The idea that hate was not a factor [in Araujo's death] is just unimaginable."[4] Because the two men had sex with Araujo, the jury decided the murder was motivated by their anger over their feeling that Araujo was biologically a man and not by a hatred of transgender people. Despite whether such offenses are officially considered hate crimes, hatred of people for their sexual orientation or gender identity is a reality of life for many LGBTQ+ individuals.

Learning and Hate

School is supposed to be a place of learning. However, for some people, it is a place that exposes them to hate for their differences. This is especially true for LGBTQ+ people, who are often cruelly mocked or physically abused because of their sexual orientation or gender identity. The 2019 National School Climate Survey by GLSEN (an organization that advocates for LBGTQ+ students) studied the experiences of LGBTQ+ students across the nation. GLSEN found that "59.1% of LGBTQ students felt unsafe at school because of their sexual orientation, 42.5% because of their gender expression, and 37.4% because of their gender."[5] The study found that 98.8 percent of LGBTQ+ students heard the word "gay" used negatively, and 91.8 percent were distressed by it. It also found that 86.3 percent of LGBTQ+ students experienced harassment or assault based on personal characteristics, such as sexual orientation, gender, gender expression, or another characteristic, such as race or disability. Although such a high number of LGBTQ+ youth faced harassment, 56.6 percent did not report it, many times because they doubted the effectiveness of intervention, and 60.5 percent said that even if they did report an incident, school staff did not respond to the problem.

Some hate crimes that happen in school are reported, but the effects of the act are no less harmful. In 2019, Grant High School in Portland,

Oregon, had hateful graffiti, including death threats, scrawled in a gender-neutral bathroom. A student at the school wrote in a Facebook post, "I am disgusted that a classmate of mine would write this. How are other queer students and I supposed to go to class knowing that the person sitting by us may think that we would be better off dead?"[6]

Many LGBTQ+ students experience hate when they attend colleges and universities. Going away to college often means new social experiences, such as living with peers in dormitories or apartments and unsupervised partying. This can open people up to new freedoms—and dangerous situations. Matthew Shepard's death is one of the most famous cases of a hate crime against an LGBTQ+ college student. Common hate crimes on college campuses involve vandalism and hate speech. In June 2020, during Pride Month at a college in Idaho, rainbow Pride flags were vandalized, and hateful comments were spray-painted on the ground. The college released a statement, saying, "As you all know, there was an ugly act of hate on our campus last night. An act of hatred against one of us is an act against all of us … This is our town and our campus and there is no place for hate here."[7]

Violence at Home and in Public

School can be a major hub of hate for LGBTQ+ students. However, sometimes people also face hate at home and in their community. In August 2020, Kendall Stephens was brutally attacked in her home in Philadelphia, Pennsylvania. The Black transgender woman was assaulted by six neighbors who had been having a fight outside her home, and they followed her inside to beat her. She suffered severe blows to the head, a fractured nose, and bruised ribs. Stephens said, "Whenever someone approaches me in any kind of way that I think might be violent, I'm thinking, is this the day that I'm going to be murdered? This is what so many of us are thinking in our minds."[8] Sometimes, LGBTQ+ individuals have their homes vandalized. In January 2017, the home of a gay couple in Van Nuys, California, was viciously vandalized—the carpets coated in bleach, pipes broken, and spray-painted slurs throughout. Being targeted at home makes people feel especially vulnerable, or open to attack, because home is where most people expect to feel safe.

LGBTQ+ individuals are also sometimes targeted while out in public. In June 2019, a gay couple was attacked in Washington, D.C., while walking together down a street at night. Their attacker yelled a gay slur before attacking, and others joined in to beat the couple. In August 2020, three transgender women were robbed and assaulted on Hollywood Boulevard in Los Angeles, California. The attacker threatened the women with a crowbar, beat them, and made hateful remarks about their gender identity. Bystanders taunted the women and laughed, as the moment was caught on film. One of the women, Joslyn Flawless, said in an Instagram post after the attack that it was the "scariest moment" of her life. She recalled, "He said if I was trans he would kill me."[9]

Terrorizing Transgender Individuals

Attacks against transgender people are some of the most savage hate crimes. In 2019, the American Medical Association (AMA) adopted a plan to help bring attention to the "epidemic of violence" against the transgender community. AMA Board Member S. Bobby Mukkamala, MD, said, "According to available tracking, fatal anti-transgender violence in the U.S. is on the rise and most victims were Black transgender women. The number of victims could be even higher due to underreporting and better data collection by law enforcement is needed to create strategies that will prevent anti-transgender violence."[10]

The year 2020 saw an unprecedented number of transgender or gender nonconforming people fatally shot or killed by other violent means. Most of those people were Black or Latinx transgender women. The Human Rights Campaign (HRC) has been tracking this data since 2013 but had never seen such a high number. Among those killed just in that year alone were Monika Diamond, a Black transgender woman from Charlotte, North Carolina; Dominique "Rem'mie" Fells, a Black transgender woman in Philadelphia, Pennsylvania; and Tony McDade, a Black transgender man in Tallahassee, Florida.

Prior to this, HRC published *A National Epidemic: Fatal Anti-Transgender Violence in America in 2018*. The publication attempted to answer the question "What Leads to Anti-Transgender Violence?" HRC pointed to a number of factors, including anti-trans stigma (which leads to the dehumanization of transgender people), denial of opportunity (which prevents full participation in society), and increased risk factors, such as

This transgender flag is raised in Toronto for the Transgender Day of Remembrance, which occurs every year on November 20 to honor the memory of transgender people whose lives were lost to hate crimes.

Life or Death

Violence against LGBTQ+ people is sometimes a matter of life and death, especially for transgender women of color. Physical harm may be the focus of many news stories, but the mental toll of anti-LGBTQ+ hate crimes can also be deadly. Hate speech, hateful messages, and bullying against LGBTQ+ people can lead a person to self-harm and suicide. The Trevor Project is the leading national organization providing crisis intervention and suicide prevention services to LGBTQ+ youth. The organization has a 24-hour crisis line for young people who are having scary thoughts about self-harm or suicide. The Trevor Project reported that lesbian, gay, and bisexual youth are almost five times as likely to have attempted suicide as heterosexual youth. The organization has stated, "Each episode of LGBT victimization, such as physical or verbal harassment or abuse, increases the likelihood of self-harming behavior by 2.5 times on average."[1] According to the UCLA Williams Institute's report on the 2015 U.S. Transgender Survey, nearly 98 percent of transgender respondents who had experienced four instances of discrimination and violence within that year had thought about suicide—and 51 percent of them had attempted suicide that year. Risk factors that heightened the chance of suicidal thoughts and attempts included family rejection, discrimination, and lack of access to gender-affirming medical care. The hate against LGBTQ+ youth, therefore, is often a matter of life and death.

1. "Preventing Suicide: Facts About Suicide," The Trevor Project, www.thetrevorproject.org/resources/preventing-suicide/facts-about-suicide/ (accessed November 9, 2020).

poverty, homelessness, intimate partner violence, and sexual assault. They argue that the higher rates of risk factors in turn reinforce anti-trans stigma and false narratives about transgender individuals. HRC notes that these issues are also connected to both racism and sexism.

Your Opinion Matters!

1. How can a greater understanding of gender identity and sexual orientation help prevent hate crimes?
2. How can students make their school a safe and accepting place for LGBTQ+ individuals?
3. How might dehumanization of the "other" lead to deadly violence against transgender people?

CHAPTER FIVE

TARGETING DIFFERENCES AND DISABILITIES

Some people target others just because they are different in some way. People are perceived as different for what they wear, what language they speak, or where they come from. People with physical and intellectual disabilities or mental illnesses are not just seen as different—they are often seen as "easy targets." Some people are also more vulnerable to attack because of immigration status or homelessness. People who are perceived as different face hate speech, humiliation, and even physical assault—and sometimes it's considered a hate crime.

Hated for Disabilities

The 2019 FBI hate crimes report showed that hate crime offenses stemming from disability bias were on the rise. There were 170 reported hate crimes for disability bias that year, compared to 128 in 2017. Of those hate crimes in 2019, 117 were against people with mental disabilities, and 53 were against people with physical disabilities—and the numbers are likely much higher. The SPLC calls crimes against people with disabilities "the invisible hate crime." According to the article "The Invisible Hate Crime," by Debra McKinney, published in the Fall 2018 *Intelligence Report*

Some people have misconceptions about people with disabilities when they have limited experience with them. For example, they may assume someone in a wheelchair cannot do well in school. In reality, every individual has their own abilities and needs, and many succeed in education with the right supports.

by the SPLC, "People with disabilities are at least 2.5 times more likely to experience violence than those without." McKinney wrote, "Because for decades people with disabilities were often locked away in institutions or kept out of mainstream society, it created an idea that people with disabilities were 'less than.' Which is why hate crimes against people with disabilities are often minimized and called pranks or bullying instead of referring to them as what they are, hate crimes."[1]

People without disabilities sometimes see people with disabilities as less than human, which is a major contributor to hate and violence against these people. The language people use around disability can make this worse. For example, if you refer to someone as "that blind woman," "that schizophrenic man," or "that Down syndrome kid," it puts their disability before their personhood. Rather, you should use "person-first" language, which restores a person's humanity, by referring to someone as "a woman with visual impairment," "a man with schizophrenia," or "a kid with Down syndrome."

Person-first language and campaigns against hate crimes based on disability can help empower people to report hate crimes. Sam Ross, a Scottish woman with Down syndrome, was spat on by a man as she waited for her train in Glasgow. As part of the Don't Tolerate Hate campaign, she said, "I didn't report it to police myself as I didn't know it was a crime but when I told my dad we reported it. I just don't want this to happen to anyone else, which is why I wanted to be part of this campaign. I want people to report hate crime to police."[2]

Intellectual disabilities make people more vulnerable to attack, either because they rely on certain services or are trusting of people who have malicious intent. In "The Invisible Hate Crime," McKinney said that people with intellectual disabilities are sexually assaulted at a rate seven times higher than those without intellectual disabilities. Hate crimes against people with intellectual disabilities also include beatings and murder. In 2010, 30-year-old Jennifer Daugherty was murdered by a group of people who took advantage of her intellectual disabilities. On her way to a medical appointment, six people stopped Daugherty and claimed to be her friends so she'd go with them. They spent two days torturing and humiliating her in an apartment before stabbing her and choking her with Christmas lights. Sociologist Jack Levin responded to the brutality of this crime, saying, "There are people very hostile toward people with disabilities. The sadism indicates some kind of need to feel powerful and special and important by targeting someone seen as inferior."[3]

Physical disabilities can present very clear characteristics of being "different," which can lead to mocking. During Donald Trump's 2016 presidential campaign, he mocked Serge Kovaleski, a Pulitzer Prize-winning reporter, for his physical disability—arthrogryposis—which makes him hold his hand in a different way. This kind of mocking or contempt for people's disabilities can also lead to violent actions. Some people with physical disabilities, such as blindness and deafness, or those confined to a wheelchair, may have trouble fighting back against assailants. Their disability may also be used against them if they are unable to accurately identify what happened, so the assailant can get away with their attack. In 2018, a surveillance camera caught a New York woman who was casing the apartment of a visually impaired man to try and steal from him. Nicole Jorwic, director of rights policy at The Arc of the United States (America's largest advocacy organization for people with intellectual or developmental disabilities), said, "This case highlights that there are individuals who take advantage of perceived vulnerabilities of people with disabilities. And that needs to be called out and prosecuted as a hate crime so we can continue to improve the status of individuals with disabilities in our community."[4]

Mental illness can also make people vulnerable to attack. In December 2016, four Black teenagers from Chicago, Illinois, filmed themselves torturing an 18-year-old white man with schizophrenia and attention-deficit/hyperactivity disorder (ADHD). During the attack, the assailants forced the victim to make statements related to race. However, the crime was believed to be motivated not by racism, but by hatred against those with disabilities. The young man was beaten, robbed, cut with a knife, and humiliated by being forced to drink toilet water. This brutal assault was posted on Facebook by the perpetrators as a way of bragging about their crime. This video led to their arrest, after which they were all charged with kidnapping, assault, and hate crimes. If it had not been for the video, in this and similar cases, hate crimes targeting people with disabilities and mental illness might not be brought to light.

Immigrants Face Hate

Xenophobia is a fear of foreigners. Hate crimes against immigrants are nothing new in the United States. Many groups from around the world were first targeted when they began immigrating to the new country, including the Irish, Italian, Chinese, and now, most commonly, Latinx peoples. Those who are immigrants or are perceived to be immigrants because of their skin color or the way they speak are often targets, simply because they are different. Hate crimes against immigrants are also motivated by the fear that they will weaken or alter their new homeland economically, politically, or culturally.

In 2018, Sergio Reyes and two other Mexican immigrants were at work landscaping when a man started yelling racial slurs and threatening them. The man was later acquitted of charges against him. Reyes said, "It doesn't matter if I become an American citizen. If your skin color is not white and your English is not perfect, you don't blend. Bottom line."[5] Despite the FBI's statistics, it is believed that many more hate crimes were committed against Latinx people, but these crimes were not officially reported. Many Latinx people do not report such offenses because they or members of their family are undocumented immigrants, and they fear they could be deported, or sent back to their country of origin. It is this controversy over the legal status of immigrants, particularly Latinx, that has ignited most of these hate crimes.

At a public park in Tucson, Arizona, on May 6, 2006, people were celebrating Cinco de Mayo, which commemorates the victory of Mexican forces over occupying French troops in 1862. The peaceful gathering was interrupted by members of the Border Guardians, an anti-immigration group led by Roy Warden. With a pistol strapped to his leg, Warden told the gathered Latinx people, "Listen up, Mexican invaders. We will not permit you, the ignorant, the savage, the unwashed, to

These New Yorkers peacefully rallied against anti-immigrant sentiments from Donald Trump in 2017.

Understanding Immigration

One of the keys to decreasing hate around an issue or group of people is increasing understanding around it. A 2020 Pew Research Center report compiled important facts and numbers behind the immigration issue in the United States. They found that the foreign-born population of the United States was 44.8 million in 2018. The top country of origin is Mexico; about a quarter of all U.S. immigrants come from Mexico. Immigrants from Asian countries account for 28 percent of immigrants, with large numbers coming from China, India, and the Philippines. While Hispanic (Spanish-speaking) immigrants are the largest group in the United States today, Asians are projected to become the largest immigrant group by 2055. Nearly half of the immigrants in the United States live within either California, Texas, or Florida. About 77 percent of immigrants are in the United States legally, either as temporary residents, permanent residents, or naturalized citizens. Immigrants who wish to become naturalized have to meet certain requirements and apply for citizenship.

Most Americans have positive views of immigrants. About two-thirds say immigrants strengthen the country through their hard work and talents. However, about a quarter of Americans say immigrants burden the country by taking jobs, housing, and health care.

overrun us … If any invader tries to take this land from us we will wash this land and nurture our soil with oceans of their blood!"[6] Warden later sent a threatening email to Isabel Garcia, a Tucson public defender who headed Derechos Humanos, a Latinx human-rights group. The email was titled, "Warden to Isabel Garcia: I will blow your … head off!"[7]

Anti-immigrant sentiment seemed to increase after the 2016 presidential election, and the numbers of hate crimes reported likely do not come close to the actual number of anti-immigrant hate crimes, since immigrants worry they will not be believed or they will be deported. Monica Bauer, director of Hispanic affairs at the ADL, said, "In immigrant communities, the fear is palpable. It's so much fear that I think the word doesn't really convey. It's almost terrified, like it's beyond fear. It's paralyzing fear."[8]

Many anti-immigrant attackers are fearful or angry about undocumented immigrants, so they target anyone who seems to be an immigrant. This seemed especially true with the 2019 El Paso shooting, in which the shooter railed against the "Hispanic invasion of Texas" in a social media post. However, this is often very misplaced anger. Janice Iwama, a sociology researcher and professor at the University of Massachusetts in Boston, said a common misperception is that all Latinx people are immigrants. However, the majority are actually natural-born citizens.

Hate for the Homeless

Another population that is vulnerable to hate crime attacks are people experiencing homelessness. The National Coalition for the Homeless (NCH) reported that in 2015, there were 77 attacks against homeless people, including 27 that resulted in death. That was a decrease from 122 attacks in 2014, when 26 people were killed. However, in the first week of July 2016 alone, four men were attacked, two of whom were set on fire.

In 2020 (before the COVID-19 pandemic hit the United States in full force), the National Alliance to End Homelessness released a report on the state of homelessness in the United States. In 2019, there were 567,715 people experiencing homelessness, and many of those people were unsheltered. Unsheltered means sleeping outside or in places not meant for human habitation. A large number of people experiencing homelessness are doing so as a family. The Hate Crimes Statistics Act of 1990 did not include homeless people, but that was amended by the Hate Crimes Against the Homeless Statistics Act.

Attacks against people experiencing homelessness are often brutal and even deadly. In May 2016, an elderly man who was homeless was found floating in a pond in San Francisco, California, after a deadly beating. In July 2016, a man experiencing homelessness was set on fire while sleeping in Yuma, Arizona. In February 2017, a man who was homeless was intentionally hit by a car in Riverside, California. People who are homeless sometimes also suffer bias surrounding their gender,

The homeless population in some cities, such as Los Angeles, is on the rise, which leaves more people vulnerable to violence.

Vulnerable to Hate

The NCH published their report *Vulnerable to Hate: A Survey of Bias-Motivated Violence Against People Experiencing Homelessness in 2016–2017* in December 2018. They reported that, over the course of 18 years, the NCH had compiled 1,769 reported acts of violence committed against individuals experiencing homelessness across 48 states, Puerto Rico, and Washington, D.C. Of those, 476 people died from the attacks. In 2016 alone, there were 83 documented attacks against people who were homeless and 37 deaths.

Attackers were generally males under the age of 30. The report stated:

> *While the motive for each attack was not always evident from the information available, in many cases, there was confirmation that these violent acts were perpetrated because of a bias against the victim's housing status. Other acts were deemed opportunistic and committed merely because the victim, due to their lack of housing, was in a vulnerable position.*[1]

1. *Vulnerable to Hate: A Survey of Bias-Motivated Violence Against People Experiencing Homelessness in 2016-2017*. (Washington, DC: National Coalition for the Homeless, 2018), p. 5.

race, or a disability. Like undocumented immigrants and people with disabilities, people who experience homelessness are at an increased risk of hate crimes—ones that quite often go unreported.

Your Opinion Matters!

1. How might mental illness make people more vulnerable to hate crimes?
2. How has disinformation and hate speech about immigrants affected the hate crimes against them in recent years?
3. How can the government and other organizations make homeless people less vulnerable to hate crimes?

PROUD BROTHER
IMPERIAL OFFICER
KU KLUX KLAN
REALM OF
KENTUCKY

CHAPTER SIX

WHO COMMITS HATE CRIMES?

When you read about brutal hate crimes and offensive hate speech, you might wonder who would do something like that. Just as every victim is an individual, every criminal has a story. Some are involved in hate groups and mostly post their hate online, while others go out of their way to commit violent acts against vulnerable people. Many perpetrators of hate crimes are young; in fact, according to the FBI *Hate Crime Statistics*, 15.4 percent of offenders in 2019 were under 18 years old. In order to prevent hate crimes, it is important to understand what drives those who commit them.

Arno Michaelis was once the poster person for hate. He started as an angry teenager who listened to white power music. At 17, he became involved in the white supremacist movement and helped found the Hammerskins, which became the largest racist skinhead organization in the world. He roamed the streets with his friends, beating up people of color or white anti-racists whom he accused of being "race traitors." He wrote, "By the time I turned 16, I was an alcoholic and very comfortable with hate and violence … I discovered racist skinhead music through the punk scene and learned that the swastika is an effective way of angering others—the hostility I radiated was reflected by the people around me, validating the paranoid ideology that had become my identity."[1]

Many hate groups carry the Confederate flag, which was the flag used by the Confederacy (South) during the American Civil War. Many see this as a symbol of racism, since the Confederacy fought to keep slavery.

Like many perpetrators of hate-filled violence, Michaelis was a young man who had a lot of anger and loneliness. He connected with others who gave him someone to blame for how he was feeling. After the birth of his daughter and after one of his skinhead friends was killed as a result of gang activity, he realized he would either end up in prison or dead if he continued down his current path. Not wanting to leave his daughter without a father, he began the process of leaving the racist gang. By understanding the *why* and the *who* behind a hate crime, there might be hope for changing a perpetrator's path—or at least protecting their possible victims.

Uniting Through Hate Groups

Membership in hate groups surged during the early 21st century. The two most common factors that hate-crime perpetrators share are youth and a link to a hate group. The Intelligence Project by the SPLC tracks the activities of hate groups and publishes *The Intelligence Report* with their findings. The center reported that in 2016, there were 917 active U.S. hate groups. By 2019, there were 940 hate groups in the United States. There was a 55 percent increase in white nationalist hate groups since 2017 and a 43 percent increase in anti-LGBTQ+ hate groups just in 2019. These hate groups spread hate speech, and many of them advocate violence against Black people, Jews, Muslims, Latinx people, and LGBTQ+ individuals. A few of them even commit hate crimes.

The surge in hate group membership might be attributed to the internet and social media. These outlets help extremists spread conspiracy theories and messages of racism and hate. Many hate groups meet primarily online and share their ideas and even assaults in this online space. The shooters in the Christchurch massacre in New Zealand and the El Paso shooting in Texas both posted "manifestos" online before they attacked.

The SPLC defines a hate group as "an organization that—based on its official statements or principles, the statements of its leaders, or its activities—has beliefs or practices that attack or malign an entire class of people, typically for their immutable characteristics."[2] It places hate groups under a few major categories: neo-Nazi, white nationalist, Ku Klux Klan (KKK), racist skinhead, Christian Identity, neo-Confederate, Black separatist, anti-immigrant, anti-Muslim, and anti-LGBTQ+. They also have a category of "General Hate" that includes hate music, Holocaust denial, and radical traditional Catholicism. Many hate groups came together for the 2017 "Unite the Right" rally in Charlottesville, Virginia, which was one of the largest, most violent gatherings in the United States in recent history. It brought together hate groups including neo-Nazi, KKK, and alt-right organizations.

The KKK is the oldest surviving white nationalist group in the United States. KKK groups make up a large portion of hate groups in the United States. The KKK started at the end of the American Civil War to intimidate Southern Black people after slavery had ended. They wanted to keep Black people from exercising their basic civil rights and often brutally attacked them by lynching, rape, and even tar-and-feathering. They became known for wearing hooded costumes and burning crosses. The KKK opposed Catholic and Jewish immigration in the 1920s and reared up violently in the 1960s to oppose the civil rights movement. Although the KKK lost steam in the following decades, there are still between 5,000 and 8,000 KKK members between different organizations. In 2016, the KKK had an estimated 130 groups. In 2019, the American Christian Dixie Knights of the Ku Klux Klan saw the greatest increase in membership.

Neo-Nazi groups idolize Nazi Germany and Adolf Hitler, and they hate Jews. One of the largest neo-Nazi groups in the country is the

KKK members are known for wearing white robes and hoods.

Alt-Right Hate

The alternative right—frequently called the alt-right for short—is a set of far-right ideologies, groups, and individuals who believe that white identity is under attack. The alt-right says multiculturalism threatens to undermine white people and their civilization with social justice and political correctness.

Richard Bertrand Spencer was an alt-right celebrity and head of the National Policy Institute, a white nationalist organization. He first used the term "Alternative Right" in 2008. He sees immigration as a "last stand" for white Americans, and has said, "Our dream is a new society, an ethno-state that would be a gathering point for all Europeans. It would be a new society based on very different ideals than, say, the Declaration of Independence."[1] Many people who consider themselves part of the alt-right use the internet to post things that are racist, sexist, or anti-immigrant. Not all members of the alt-right believe the same things, but most believe in preserving their idea of white identity. For this reason, most oppose letting non-white people immigrate to the United States. *The New York Times* attempted to define their views:

> *There is no obvious catchall word for them. The word "racist" has been stretched to cover an attitude toward biology, a disposition to hate, and a varying set of policy preferences, from [racial profiling in] policing to repatriating [deporting] illegal immigrants. While everyone in this set of groups is racist in at least one of these senses, many are not racist in others. Not many … favored the term "white supremacist." The word implies a claim to superiority—something few insisted on. "White nationalist" is closer to the mark; most people in this part of the alt-right think whites either ought to have a nation or constitute one already. But they feel that almost all words tend to misdescribe or stigmatize them.*[2]

The alt-right often uses the internet for widespread propaganda campaigns around hashtags such as #WhiteGenocide and #ISaluteWhitePeople. Many see Donald Trump as an alt-right hero because of his fight against political correctness and his attitude toward people of other races. They have their own news websites, publishing houses, and even a yearly official gathering in Washington, D.C.

1. "Richard Bertrand Spencer," Southern Poverty Law Center, www.splcenter.org/fighting-hate/extremist-files/individual/richard-bertrand-spencer-0 (accessed November 9, 2020).

2. Christopher Caldwell, "What the Alt-Right Really Means," *New York Times*, December 2, 2016, www.nytimes.com/2016/12/02/opinion/sunday/what-the-alt-right-really-means.html.

A National Socialist Movement (NSM) rally took place outside of the U.S. Capitol on April 19, 2008.

National Socialist Movement (NSM). It started in 1959 as the American Nazi Party. NSM became known for large protests, in which members wore swastikas and Nazi uniforms. In 2019, NSM lost its leader—Jeff Schoep—who had led the group for more than 20 years. He claimed to have renounced his racist views. However, neo-Nazi groups, such as the National Alliance, continue to spread hate online.

There are also many smaller hate groups in the United States. In the early 21st century, organizations such as the Border Guardians and Texas Minutemen were created to oppose undocumented immigration. Felon Larry Hopkins started a border militia called the United Constitutional Patriots in 2018 which is stationed on the U.S.-Mexican border to detain migrants who cross into the United States. Some people have joined these groups because they hate all Mexicans, even those who are U.S. citizens.

The Westboro Baptist Church (WBC) in Topeka, Kansas, is an extremist church known for its hate speech against LGBTQ+ people, Catholics, Jews, Muslims, several other minority religions, U.S. soldiers, and politicians. In protests at the funerals of soldiers killed in the Iraq War, members carried signs that read, "Thank God for Dead Soldiers." They claimed the deaths were a punishment from God because the United States tolerates homosexuality. The protests

These young people are shown participating in a hateful protest in front of the U.S. Supreme Court, holding signs with messages that include "Thank God for Dead Soldiers."

were universally condemned because they added to the suffering of the families and friends who were already mourning the deaths of loved ones.

How do hate groups find supporters? One strategy is to get media coverage. A group might host a major event or demonstration, such as the 2017 "Unite the Right" demonstration. Today, however, the internet is the best medium for young members. Many young people visit hate websites and social media pages out of idle curiosity about such groups or because of a fascination with the symbols they use, such as the Nazi swastika. Hate groups welcome young people, who are often too naive to understand that the racist and hateful messages their websites present are based on lies and faulty stereotypes.

Young white males are often recruited by hate groups online.

Hate groups also try to recruit young people with "white power" and "hatecore" music. Hate music was especially important with the racist skinhead youth culture of the 1980s and 1990s. Skinheads were violent, often young, white supremacists, known for their shaved heads, Doc Martens boots, and racist tattoos. There are still skinhead groups today, but young people have moved more toward white nationalist groups and militant neo-Nazi groups.

In March 1995, the Stormfront White Nationalist Community started the first hate website. The website was created by Don Black, a former Klansman who believed the new technology would allow hate groups to easily communicate with many more people. Stormfront is no longer alone in spreading hatred. Today, there are too many websites, forums, and social media pages to keep track of. They have a wide reach, as people can easily make or join a group, share their messages, and encourage others to repost them. In June 2020, Facebook removed nearly 200 social media accounts that were linked to white supremacist groups planning to encourage members to militarize against Black Lives Matter protests. These accounts were tied to two hate groups already banned on the platform—the Proud Boys and the American Guard. It remains to be seen how social media sites will deal with a rise in hate group organization and the spread of disinformation from hate groups online. The FBI says violent extremist groups also use internet games and apps to find new recruits.

Some skinheads had tattoos that showed their hate group affiliation.

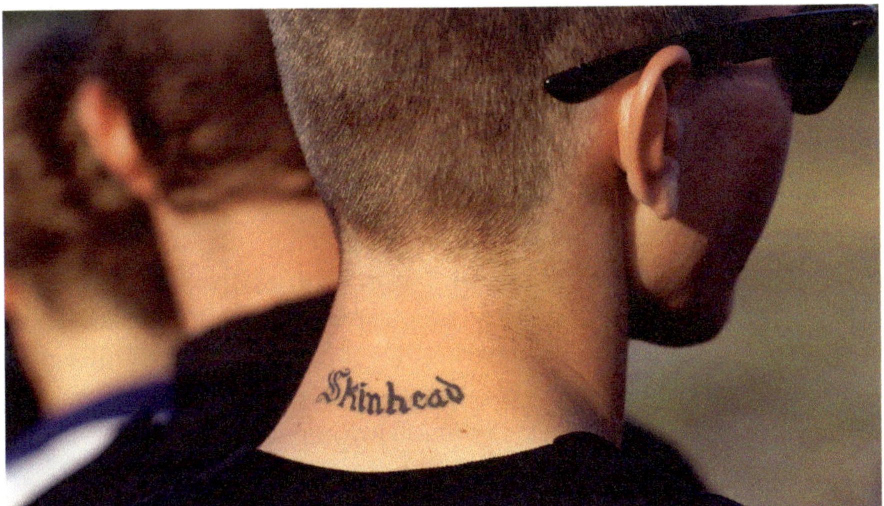

There are certain signs you can watch out for that might indicate a violent extremist organization. They might say their cause justifies the use of violence; use hateful words against a certain race, religion, gender, or ethnic group; or try to pick out religious passages to justify hatred and violence. For some people, these signs are not red flags signaling something dangerous—they are welcome signs from a new community. Psychologist Ervin Staub tried to make sense of hate group involvement:

> *Why would people join groups like that? It usually involves them finding no other socially acceptable and meaningful ways to fulfill important needs—the need for identity; the need for a feeling of effectiveness; the need for a feeling of connection ... Often, these are people who don't feel like they've succeeded or had a chance to succeed across normal channels of success in society. They may come from families that are problematic or families where they're exposed to this kind of extreme view of white superiority and nationalism. If you don't feel you have much influence and power in the world, you get a sense of power from being part of a community and especially a rather militant community.*[3]

Police Brutality

Young people commit many hate crimes each year, but older adults also commit hate crimes. Some adults who commit hate crimes are in positions of authority—even law enforcement. While many law enforcement officials are "good cops" who want the best for the communities they serve, there have been many high-profile cases of police officers using unwarranted and even deadly force based on bias. Some studies suggest that this is a problem that often goes unreported.

This issue came to light on the national stage during protests in response to the police killings of Tamir Rice, Michael Brown, and Eric Garner, but it seemed everything came to a head in 2020. That year, massive protests were sparked by the brutal police killing of George Floyd, an unarmed Black man in Minneapolis, Minnesota. Floyd's brutal murder sparked demonstrations in all 50 U.S. states and Washington, D.C., as well as in cities around the world. People marched for justice in the face of police brutality and even made calls to defund the police. This means decreasing police budgets and using some of the money for essential social services, such as those focused on mental health, education, addiction treatment, and recreation centers.

The difference between how law enforcement treats white people and people of color was demonstrated in 2020 and 2021. When Black Lives Matter protesters took to the streets in the summer of 2020, many protesters were met with an aggressive, militarized police presence. Just months later, on January 6, 2021, armed white attackers descended on the U.S. Capitol, incited by President Trump. Law enforcement was lacking and did not stop the attackers from getting inside the Capitol and nearly harming senators and congresspeople. Javad Khazaeli, a lawyer representing some Black Lives Matter protesters, said of the U.S. Capitol attack, "It couldn't be a more perfect example for everybody to see the two different criminal justice systems we have in America."[4]

Percent saying each of the following has happened to them because of their race or ethnicity since the coronavirus outbreak

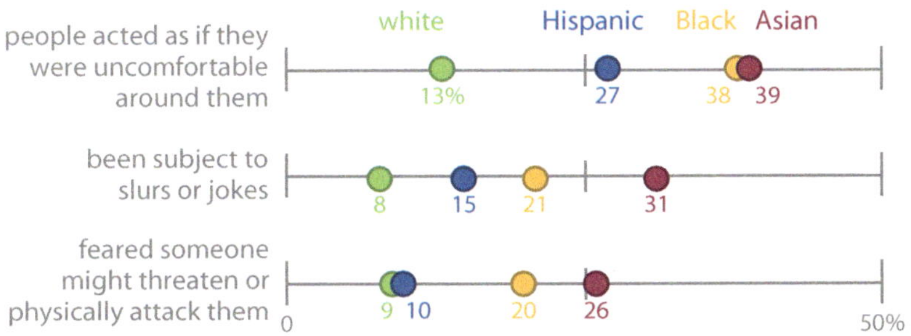

The year 2020 was full of racial tension and uncertainty over issues that included the COVID-19 pandemic. The Pew Research Center found that Asian and Black Americans were more likely than other groups to report negative experiences because of their ethnicity or race since the pandemic began.

A Year of Racial Reckoning

The year 2020 was a reckoning moment in U.S. history. The COVID-19 pandemic had disproportionately affected Black communities, and several police killings made people around the country take up the fight against systemic racism. NAACP President Derrick Johnson explained systemic racism as "systems and structures that have procedures or processes that disadvantage African Americans."[1] It is seen in employment, housing, health care, education, and the criminal justice system.

On May 25, police officers arrested George Floyd in Minneapolis. A convenience store owner called the police after suspecting Floyd had used a counterfeit, or fake, 20-dollar bill to buy cigarettes. Witness videos show one of the white policemen, Derek Chauvin, pinning Floyd to the ground with a knee to his neck. Chauvin knelt on George Floyd's neck for more than eight minutes, even after Floyd had passed out. Three other officers looked on. Many people saw this as a murder, and even a hate crime. It enraged people around the world, who also pointed to the brutal March 2020 killing of Breonna Taylor. Taylor was a 26-year-old Black emergency medical technician (EMT). Police allegedly attempted to enter her apartment without announcing themselves while she was in bed, using a no-knock warrant based on her ex-boyfriend's drug case. When her startled boyfriend fired a warning shot, police proceeded to shoot blindly into the apartment, hitting Taylor at least eight times. She was given no medical attention, though she struggled to breathe, and she died. The deaths of Breonna Taylor and George Floyd left the Black community enraged and deeply hurt.

Black Lives Matter responded to Floyd's death on their website:

> *George Floyd couldn't breathe. We can't either. We live in fear. Fear of walking outside. Wearing a hoodie. Going for a jog. Sleeping in our own home. Existing. Every day, a new hashtag. Every hour, a new injustice. Every second, more pain. We don't deserve to live like this—and we continue to fight until white supremacy no longer permeates every corner of this country—until we can live full lives—freely.*[2]

Police brutality toward minorities is nothing new. Many argue that law enforcement as we know it evolved out of attempts to "protect" white U.S. citizens from Native Americans and to keep

Black Lives Matter protests occurred in nearly every major city in the summer of 2020. Although an overwhelming majority of demonstrations were peaceful, a few involved violence and looting. Police used their power to arrest those who were rioting; however, even peaceful protests were often met with militarized attacks by police. In October 2020, *The Guardian* reported that there had been around 1,000 instances of police brutality documented since the anti-racism protests had begun, including attacks on medics and journalists and use of tear gas and rubber bullets. Melina Abdullah, co-founder of Black Lives Matter Los Angeles, said, "Black Lives Matter has now been recognized as the largest social movement in global history and that scares people … That scares folks who are invested in making the world more racist, not less and making the world oppressive not less and folks who are tethered to a system of policing that's oppressive and brutal and violent."[3]

Thousands of people joined in a silent protest walk across the Brooklyn Bridge on the day that George Floyd was buried in 2020.

1. Quoted in N'dea Yancey-Bragg, "What is Systemic Racism? Here's What it Means and How You Can Help Dismantle It," *USA Today*, June 15, 2020, www.usatoday.com/story/news/nation/2020/06/15/systemic-racism-what-does-mean/5343549002/.

2. "Rest in Power, Beautiful," *Black Lives Matter*, blacklivesmatter.com/rest-in-power-beautiful/ (accessed October 25, 2020).

3. Daniel Villarreal. "More Than 1,000 Black Lives Matter Protesters Harmed by Police as Public Support for Racial Justice Movement Decreases," *Newsweek*, October 29, 2020, newsweek.com/more-1000-black-lives-matter-protesters-harmed-police-public-support-racial-justice-movement-1543410.

enslaved people, and later free Black people, from enjoying basic civil rights as citizens. Many southern police departments began as slave patrols.

Many cases of police brutality against minorities have gone unreported in U.S. history. However, once people were able to film violent police encounters, they received the attention they deserved. One infamous case involved Rodney King, a Black man, who, on March 3, 1991, was brutally attacked by Los Angeles police officers when they arrested him for speeding. The officers claimed that King was resisting arrest and that they were only doing what was necessary to subdue him. The incident, however, had been videotaped by a bystander. When it was shown on television, it created a firestorm of controversy about police brutality. In 1992, when the four officers charged with using excessive force to subdue King were found not guilty, Black people in Los Angeles were so angry that they erupted in one of the city's worst riots.

The King beating was one of many videotaped incidents involving white officers who appeared to use excessive force when arresting African Americans. Many of those incidents have resulted in the death of the victims. In July 2014, Eric Garner, a Black man, was killed by police as they arrested him. Garner was put in a chokehold, even though he was not behaving violently and, despite telling the officers several times that he could not breathe, was not given medical attention afterward. An autopsy—a medical examination conducted to determine the cause of a person's death—showed that the chokehold and pressure to the chest were responsible for Garner's death. The arresting officers defended their actions, but after viewing video of the incident that had been taken with an onlooker's cell phone, many people believed the police had used excessive force and ignored Garner's pleas for help. Garner's last words—"I can't breathe"—became a rallying cry for Black Lives Matter.

Police are more likely to hurt or shoot an unarmed Black person than a white one because of fears that the Black person is more likely to become violent. Many unarmed Black people, especially Black men, have been shot when police mistakenly believed the victim was reaching for a gun. These fears are based on racist beliefs that police officers may not even be entirely aware of, but they influence behavior nonetheless. Some people say race is not an issue in these

In June 2020, then-Senator Kamala Harris and Senator Cory Booker introduced the Justice in Policing Act of 2020 which sought to hold police accountable, change the culture of law enforcement, and build trust between communities and police.

cases because police also shoot unarmed white people. However, as the *Chicago Tribune* reported in July 2016:

> *According to the most recent census data, there are nearly 160 million more white people in America than there are black people. White people make up roughly 62 percent of the U.S. population but only about 49 percent of those who are killed by police officers. African Americans, however, account for 24 percent of those fatally shot and killed by the police despite being just 13 percent of the U.S. population. As The Post noted in a new analysis published last week, that means black Americans are 2.5 times as likely as white Americans to be shot and killed by police officers … And, when considering shootings confined within a single race, a black person shot and killed by police is more likely to have been unarmed than a white person. About 13 percent of all black people who have been fatally shot by police since January 2015 were unarmed, compared with 7 percent of all white people.*[5]

Native Americans also face violence from police, although this issue often goes unreported by the media. In many of these instances, the police are not charged with a crime. People of all races have recently begun campaigning for police reform and accountability; they want police who use excessive force to be charged with assault or murder.

Another group discriminated against—and even targeted—by law enforcement officials is the LGBTQ+ community. According to a 2012 National Inmate Survey, self-identified lesbian, gay, or bisexual (LGB) people are incarcerated at a rate of 1,882 per 100,000. That is three times higher than the rate of incarceration of the heterosexual U.S. adult population. The National Coalition of Anti-Violence Programs published a national report that claimed transgender people were 3.7 times more likely to experience police violence compared to cisgender survivors and victims. The report noted, "Transgender communities' experience of discriminatory and violent policing can be a barrier to accessing critical support

It is hard to know how many incidents of police violence happen every year. That is because, unless activists and journalists bring it to national attention, it is rarely reported. Police officers generally do not face legal consequences, even when they have killed a civilian.

in the aftermath of violence, placing transgender people at greater risk when they do experience violence."[6]

When a hate crime occurs, one of the most powerful things government and community leaders can do is condemn the offense. This shows offenders that their behavior is not okay, and shows victims that they are welcome and protected in their community. With some police departments requiring body cams and cell phones readily available in police encounters, these issues may continue to come to light in the coming years, and America may be forced to reckon with its history of injustice and white supremacist systems.

Your Opinion Matters!

1. Why do you think someone might join a hate group?
2. Some people respond to "Black Lives Matter" with "All Lives Matter." Why might this feel offensive to people who have dealt with systemic racism?
3. Should instances of police violence against Black individuals be considered hate crimes? Why or why not?

CHAPTER SEVEN

DRIVING OUT DARKNESS

How can the tide of hate be changed? In 1963, Dr. Martin Luther King Jr. said, "Darkness cannot drive out darkness, only light can do that. Hate cannot drive out hate, only love can do that."[1] This calls for positive action for justice and the betterment of marginalized communities.

Everyone has a role to play in preventing hate crimes, from young people to adults to organizations and lawmakers. This action is necessary because hate crimes harm so many communities across the United States and the wider world. It is important to not normalize hatred, which is a trend that has happened especially in the past few years. You can instead be an ally in the fight against prejudice.

As the United States and many other countries become more diverse in race and religion and more accepting of different gender identities and sexual orientations, there will likely be some pushback to that change by white supremacists and other hateful people. However, it is important to know that people can work together toward a more just future and stand up for acceptance and civility instead of hate.

Hate-Crime Laws

Hatred toward "the other" may never be fully solved. However, federal and state laws have the ability to keep people from acting

You can make a positive change in the world. Start with your group of friends. Who do you spend time with? Are they loving and welcoming toward people who are different, or do they normalize hate?

on their hate, or to prosecute people who do. Citizens should encourage lawmakers to keep hate-crime legislation up-to-date and make it a priority. Society's laws define what is and is not acceptable behavior. Hate-crime laws that impose strict penalties may make people think twice before attacking people on the basis of bias.

As of early 2021, most states have laws against hate crimes, except Wyoming, Arkansas, and South Carolina. In August 2020, Arkansas introduced a bill for a new law that would increase penalties in hate crime cases. All hate crimes can be reported to the FBI, even if a state does not have a specific law against hate crimes. Many state laws cover all types of hate crimes. Some states have created new criminal offenses for hate crimes, and others have simply increased penalties for existing crimes in which the offenses can also be considered hate crimes. Both types of laws result in longer jail or prison sentences. Some officials believe harsher punishment is necessary because hate crimes affect society as a whole.

In 2009, President Barack Obama signed the federal Matthew Shepard and James Byrd Jr. Hate Crimes Prevention Act. Named for victims of some of the most brutal hate crimes in the national spotlight, this law expanded the definition of hate crimes to include gender, disability, gender identity, and sexual orientation. This federal act also removed obstacles to prosecutions of race- and religion-motivated violence based on jurisdiction. In 2017, Joshua Vallum of Mississippi became the first person to be prosecuted under the federal law for a crime against a transgender person. Vallum killed his ex-girlfriend Mercedes Williamson in 2015 because she was a transgender woman and he was worried his own life would be in danger if the other members of his gang, the Latin Kings, found out he had dated her. Vallum was charged by the state of Mississippi with murder, but since Mississippi's hate-crime laws do not cover crimes against LGBTQ+ people, he was also prosecuted under the federal Hate Crimes Prevention Act.

Most state laws add extra punishment for hate crimes motivated by race, religion, or ethnicity. As of 2020, however, some states still did not include sexual orientation or gender identity as a hate-crime motivation. Most did not include people experiencing homelessness in their hate crime laws. The lack of protection for the homeless was highlighted in Los Angeles in October 2018, when a woman and a man

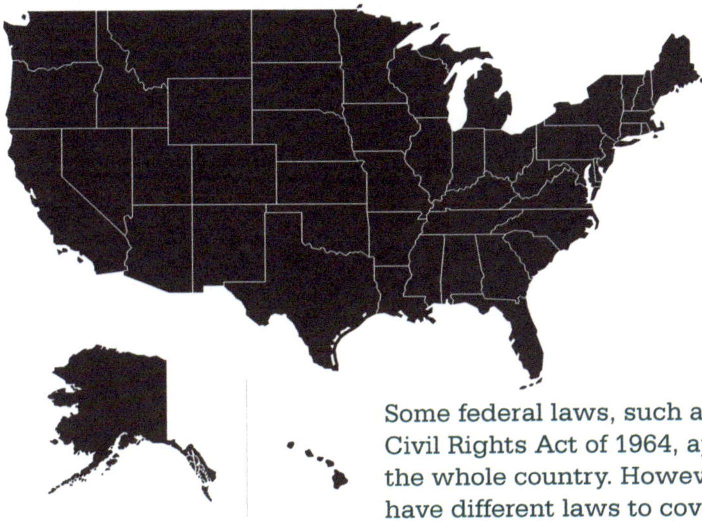

Some federal laws, such as the Civil Rights Act of 1964, apply to the whole country. However, states have different laws to cover hate crimes for different demographics.

experiencing homelessness were attacked with battery acid. Just the month before, a man was arrested for a series of attacks on people experiencing homelessness, which left four people seriously injured and four people dead across Los Angeles and Santa Monica, California.

It is important that individual states include gender identity, sexual orientation, and homelessness under their hate-crimes legislation because the federal role in prosecuting hate crimes is limited. The U.S. government does not prosecute many hate crimes because it believes that is the role of states. However, the federal government fights hate crimes by compiling hate-crime statistics, educating the public on hate crimes, and assisting hate-crime victims through agencies such as the U. S. Department of Justice's Community Relations Service.

Local governments also fight hate crimes. After the 2018 attacks against people experiencing homelessness in Los Angeles, the Los Angeles City Council considered a resolution supporting legislation that would add homeless people to the list of those protected by the state's hate-crime law.

Organizations that Fight Against Hate

The FBI collects data about hate crimes and investigates some cases. However, private organizations also use a variety of methods and

What Can Young People Do?

Many instances of hate crimes by young people are dismissed as "kids being kids," or even "boys being boys." In 2017, high school football players in Creston, Iowa, burned a cross, wore KKK hoods, and waved a Confederate flag. That same year, a group of white teens tricked an eight-year-old biracial boy into putting a rope around his neck and hung him from a tree. They left him hanging, which could have killed him. Fortunately, he survived the attack. However, he was wounded and like other hate crimes, the pain was felt by many people, not just the victim.

Hate crimes may seem like too big a problem for young people to tackle. However, it's important to know that you have more power to prevent hate crimes than you think, because they happen every day, in every place, in big and small ways. If you hear hate speech in your community or in your school, you can report it. It's never okay—and shouldn't be considered normal—for people to use hateful, discriminatory, or offensive language against another person or group because of bias. If you hear someone call another student a racial slur or homophobic slur, it can be reported. If you see someone trying to stop a student with disabilities from going about their school day, it is not just a joke. It might be a hate crime, and it should be reported to a teacher, the principal, or another trusted adult.

You might also see hate online. People are more likely to post hate speech online or attack someone virtually. You can report their behavior to the site you're using, such as Instagram or Twitter, and also report it to authorities at school or a trusted adult. Many hate groups target young people to radicalize them. If someone tries to approach you online and makes you feel uncomfortable, block them and tell a trusted adult what happened. Whether it is in person or online, you have the power to make a difference.

Respectful discussion is an important part of changing the culture of hate in your school or community.

approaches to combat hate crimes. Some have hotlines where people can report hate crimes. Some monitor hate crimes and hate groups, publish their findings, and even pursue legal action,

The SPLC has battled hate crimes since it was founded in 1971 to help Black people gain their civil rights. It monitors hate-crime activity; publicizes offenses in its quarterly magazine, the *Intelligence Report*; and uses legal action to cripple hate groups such as the KKK. In 2019, the SPLC won a federal lawsuit on behalf of Jewish real estate agent Tanya Gersh, of Whitefish, Montana, against Andrew Anglin—publisher of the extremist neo-Nazi website the Daily Stormer—for the harassing anti-Semitic threats and messages by Anglin and his followers. Anglin used his extremist website to publish 30 articles urging his followers to "troll" Gersh, and she soon received hundreds of harassing messages. Anglin published a doctored image of Gersh at a concentration camp as a threat, and Gersh developed extreme anxiety over the attacks. The SPLC's lawsuit led to $14 million in damages for Gersh. Gersh said, "This win isn't just for me, my family and my community; this is a win for everyone who has been harassed, terrorized, and bullied."[2]

Another powerful hate-crime opponent is the ADL, which was founded in 1913. It has one of the most comprehensive and informative hate-crime websites, and it monitors hate crimes through its many local offices. The ADL is one of many organizations that directly represent groups of people who are targeted for hate crimes. Other organizations include the American-Arab Anti-Discrimination Committee, the NAACP, the Asian American Legal Defense and Education Fund, and Parents and Friends of Lesbians and Gays.

Groups such as the ADL, the Council on American-Islamic Relations, and Lambda Legal also help victims cope with hate crimes. The groups help victims report hate crimes to the authorities, and many operate hate-crime hotlines. The groups also provide medical assistance and counseling for victims and advise them of their legal rights, such as what to do if their attacker is arrested and charged with the crime. These organizations empower victims of hate crimes to have their voice heard and to seek justice.

Can Hate Crime Offenders Be Reformed?

It might seem as if hate crime offenders and members of hate groups will remain hateful forever. It may seem as if the hate is so engrained into them that they could not change. However, there are a number of people who have been reformed through education and life experience. Arno Michaelis, the skinhead mentioned earlier, left his hate group behind. In 2010, he launched an online publication called Life After Hate. In 2011, Michaelis and other reformed extremists—Sammy Rangel, Angela King, Christian Picciolini, Tony McAleer, and Frank Meeink—started collaborating on a new project called Life After Hate, which turned into an anti-hate non-profit organization. Life After Hate has spoken out against extremist groups, led research into radicalization and violent extremism, and helped identify and defuse potentially violent extremists online.

Christian Picciolini is a reformed skinhead and one of the founders of Life After Hate. He gave this advice to people confronted with a white supremacist: "See the child and not the monster. It doesn't matter if that child is 16 or 60. I listen not for the ideological words. I filter those out and pay attention to what the real motivation is, and then I address that."[1] Picciolini was only 14 when he was radicalized as a skinhead. He was looking for a community who would accept him and a purpose and became a leader in his white

Educating Against Hate

In November 2017, Daryl Davis took the stage at TEDxCharlottesville and said, "Ignorance breeds fear. If we don't keep that fear in check, that fear, in turn, will breed hatred because we hate those things that frighten us. If we do not keep that hatred in check, that hatred will breed destruction."[3] Daryl Davis is a Black blues musician, and he has also spent more than 30 years befriending KKK members and convincing them to give up their robes. One of the main takeaways from Davis's work is this: People can learn to hate, but people can also learn their way out of hate through respectful dialogue.

supremacist group. He says that compassion allowed him to question those white supremacist beliefs.

When asked how an average person can help dismantle the white supremacy movement, Picciolini responded, "Make good happen. We have to embody the change that we want in this world. We have to find a way to muster compassion for the people that we think are the most undeserving of it. In all honesty, that's the only thing I've seen break hate."[2]

Christian Picciolini is shown here speaking at an event after the violence that took place in Charlottesville in 2017.

1. Quoted in Leah Wankum, "Reformed White Supremacists Share Their Stories of Healing, Compassion and Forgiveness," Shawnee Mission Post, April 12, 2019, shawneemissionpost.com/2019/04/12/reformed-white-supremacists-share-their-stories-of-healing-compassion-and-forgiveness-78361/.

2. Quoted in Wankum, "Reformed White Supremacists Share Their Stories of Healing, Compassion and Forgiveness."

Education and respectful discussion are not only tools for reforming white supremacists and hate crime offenders, however. Anti-hate groups use education in the fight against ignorance and indifference. These groups maintain websites; print publications; and sponsor speeches, lectures, and other public events. These educational efforts are aimed at the general public, but also at law enforcement officials and teachers.

An educational program that has helped entire communities fight hate crimes is Not In Our Town (NIOT). In 1993, in Billings, Montana, white supremacists desecrated a Jewish cemetery, painted swastikas on a Native American family's house, and broke a window in the home of a family displaying a menorah, which is a Jewish religious symbol. The hate spree lasted several weeks and spurred city officials and community groups to fight back in a collective effort that eventually became NIOT. A labor union painted over the swastikas, and civic organizations staged marches and protests against racism. When the *Billings Gazette* printed pictures of paper menorahs, 10,000 people of all faiths displayed them in their windows. In 1995, the Public Broadcasting Service (PBS) televised a documentary about Billings titled *Not In Our Town*. Since then, the documentary has inspired people in hundreds of other communities to band together to fight hate crimes. Today, The Working Group organization runs the Not in Our Town project. This movement aims to stop hate, address bullying, and build safe, inclusive communities for all by using social media, film, and organizing tools. Not in Our Town reaches out to schools, communities, and law enforcement with educational resources to prevent intolerance.

Teaching Tolerance is a project from the SPLC, which aims to "help teachers and schools educate children and youth to be active participants in a diverse democracy."[4] It provides free resources to educators, which emphasize social justice and fight bias. Films, publications, and curriculums from Teaching Tolerance are part of an effort to prevent the growth of hate.

Raising a Voice for Change

You cannot single-handedly dismantle a hate group or an ideology. However, you can raise a voice for change in the world. You can make an effort to be compassionate and accepting of all people and engage in respectful conversation, even with people who look and think differently from you. You can also report a hate crime if you see one happening and make sure not to normalize hateful speech or behavior.

Think about what you have been taught about people who are different from you. Do you have any "us vs. them" biases that have impacted the way you treat people? How can you push back against those biases to humanize that person or group? It is important to see people as individuals and also recognize the shared humanity between people. You can educate the people around you

Sometimes family members of hate crime victims use their voice to make change. Judy Shepard, the mother of Matthew Shepard, wrote in her book *The Meaning of Matthew*, "I feel it necessary to show the great nation that we live in that there doesn't need to be this kind of violence and hatred in our world."[5]

about hate crimes. You can also have respectful discussions with people who think differently from you. As Daryl Davis said, "Keep in mind, when two enemies are talking, they're not fighting, they're talking. They might be yelling and screaming, but at least they're talking. It's when the talking ceases that the ground becomes fertile for violence."[6]

In his book *Long Walk to Freedom*, Nelson Mandela—the first Black president of South Africa—spoke of the possibility of learning to love after hate. Even after spending 27 years in prison for working against the hate of apartheid (racial segregation), his message is a hopeful one: "No one is born hating another person because of the color of his skin, or his background, or his religion. People must learn to hate, and if they can learn to hate, they can be taught to love, for love comes more naturally to the human heart than its opposite."[7]

People can use their voice through peaceful protests and marches to tell their elected officials and their fellow citizens that they are standing up against hate.

The past few years have seen a spike in hate crimes, hate speech, and hate group activity both in person and online. However, they have also introduced an opportunity to shed light on the hate, and in doing so, to root it out. How can you meet this moment in history and be a part of the change for good?

Your Opinion Matters!

1. Why is it important to have both federal and state hate-crime laws?
2. Do you believe a hate crime offender can truly be reformed?
3. What is one thing you could do to stop hate speech or violence in your own life?

GETTING INVOLVED

The following are some suggestions for taking what you've just read and applying that information to your everyday life.

- Learn more about the history of hate crimes in the United States for different minority groups.
- Find accurate and responsible news sources to read more about extremist violence in the United States. Fact check any information you read with a reliable source.
- Look into the issues that your politicians stand for when it comes to discrimination and hate crimes. You can petition your politicians or write them a letter if you think they should do something differently.
- Attend community events that may allow you to meet people who are different from you, such as fundraising walks for people with certain disabilities or social justice events.
- Talk to people who think differently from you with respect, but do not normalize hate speech.
- Report hate speech and threats when you see them online or at school.
- Be an advocate for people who are being bullied in school. If it is not safe for you to intervene in a conflict, get a teacher or administrator involved.
- Join or start a group or club in your school where people can talk about social justice issues—for LGBTQ+ individuals, people with disabilities, and people of different races and religions.

NOTES

Introduction: "The Root of Evil Everywhere"

1. Elie Wiesel, "We Choose Honor," *Parade Magazine*, September 11, 2011, parade.com/94456/eliewiesel/elie-wiesel-we-choose-honor/.
2. "Learn About Hate Crimes," *The United States Department of Justice*, www.justice.gov/hatecrimes/learn-about-hate-crimes/chart (accessed October 24, 2020).
3. Weihua Li, "Why Police Struggle to Report One of The Fastest-Growing Hate Crimes," The Marshall Project, November 26, 2019, www.themarshallproject.org/2019/11/26/why-police-struggle-to-report-one-of-the-fastest-growing-hate-crimes.
4. The Southern Poverty Law Center, "The Year in Hate and Extremism: Rage Against Change," *The Intelligence Report*, 2019.
5. Quoted in Aberjhani, *The Wisdom of W.E.B. Dubois* (New York, NY: Citadel Press Books, 2003), p. 76.

Chapter One: The Origins of Hate

1. Jack Levin and Gordana Rabrenovic, *Why We Hate* (Amherst, NY: Prometheus Books, 2004), p. 63.
2. Marianna Pogosyan, "Understanding Hate," *Psychology Today*, November 25, 2019, www.psychologytoday.com/us/blog/between-cultures/201911/understanding-hate.
3. Robert M. Baird and Stuart E. Rosenbaum, *Hatred, Bigotry, and Prejudice: Definitions, Causes, and Solutions* (Amherst, NY: Prometheus Books, 1999), p. 13.
4. Hannah Devlin, "Human Brain Is Predisposed to Negative Stereotypes, New Study Suggests," *The Guardian*, November 1 2016, www.theguardian.com/science/2016/nov/01/human-brain-is-predisposed-to-negative-stereotypes-new-study-suggests.
5. Sara Bullard, *Teaching Tolerance: Raising Open-Minded, Empathetic Children* (New York, NY: Doubleday, 1996), p. 28.

6. Jack Levin and Jack McDevitt, *Hate Crimes Revisited: America's War Against Those Who Are Different* (Cambridge, MA: Westview, 2002), p. 27.
7. Gregory M Herek, "'Us' and 'Them' of Murder," *Los Angeles Times*, October 16, 1998, www.latimes.com/archives/la-xpm-1998-oct-16-me-33049-story.html.
8. Carl Miller, "Social Media Is Driving the Rise of Hate Crime, but It Can Also Stop It," *The Telegraph*, October 12, 2015, www.telegraph.co.uk/news/uknews/crime/11925950/Social-media-is-driving-the-rise-of-hate-crime-but-it-can-also-stop-it.html.

Chapter Two: Race-Related Hate

1. "Herstory," *Black Lives Matter*, September 7, 2019, blacklivesmatter.com/herstory/.
2. Quoted in Christina Hall, "Warren Man Faces 9 Criminal Charges in Hate Crimes against Black Family," *Detroit Free Press*, September 30, 2020, www.freep.com/story/news/local/michigan/macomb/2020/09/30/warren-man-arrested-hate-crimes/3586151001/.
3. George M. Fredrickson, *White Supremacy: Comparative Study of American and South African History* (Oxford University Press, Oxford, UK: 1981), p. xii.
4. Lilliana Byington, et al, "Black Americans Still Are Victims of Hate Crimes More than Any Other Group," *Center for Public Integrity*, August 21, 2019, publicintegrity.org/politics/black-americans-still-are-victims-of-hate-crimes-more-than-any-other-group/.
5. Byington, "Black Americans Still Are Victims of Hate Crimes More than Any Other Group."
6. Byington, "Black Americans Still Are Victims of Hate Crimes More than Any Other Group."
7. Garet Bleir, et al. "Murdered and Missing Native American Women Challenge Police and Courts," *Center for Public Integrity*, modified October 19, 2018, publicintegrity.org/politics/murdered-and-missing-native-american-women-challenge-police-and-courts/.
8. Monica Muñoz Martinez, "The 'Forgotten' History Of Anti-Latino Violence In The U.S.," Interview by Tonya Mosley. *Here and Now*, NPR and WBUR, November 25, 2019, www.wbur.org/hereandnow/2019/11/25/history-violence-against-latinos.

9. Quoted in Linda Greenhouse, "An Intense Attack by Justice Thomas on Cross-Burning," *New York Times*, December 12, 2002, www.nytimes.com/2002/12/12/us/an-intense-attack-by-justice-thomas-on-cross-burning.html.

10. Quoted in Ashley Turner, "'I Want Them to Forgive Me': Man Who Terrorized Black Family for Three Days Tells Judge He Wants Forgiveness, Claims His Actions Were 'Out of Character,'" *Atlanta Black Star*, October 4, 2020, atlantablackstar.com/2020/10/04/i-want-them-to-forgive-me-white-man-who-terrorized-black-family-for-three-days-tells-judge-he-wants-forgiveness-claims-his-actions-were-out-of-character/.

Chapter Three: Attacks Based on Religion

1. "Antisemitic Incidents Hit All-Time High in 2019," Anti-Defamation League, May 12, 2019, www.adl.org/news/press-releases/antisemitic-incidents-hit-all-time-high-in-2019.

2. Quoted in Jennifer Medina, et al., "One Dead in Synagogue Shooting Near San Diego; Officials Call It Hate Crime," *New York Times*, April 27, 2019, www.nytimes.com/2019/04/27/us/poway-synagogue-shooting.html.

3. Eric Lichtblau, "Hate Crimes Against American Muslims Most Since Post-9/11 Era," *New York Times*, September 17, 2016, www.nytimes.com/2016/09/18/us/politics/hate-crimes-american-muslims-rise.html.

4. Vikram Dodd, "Anti-Muslim Hate Crimes Soar in UK after Christchurch Shootings," *The Guardian*, March 22, 2019, www.theguardian.com/society/2019/mar/22/anti-muslim-hate-crimes-soar-in-uk-after-christchurch-shootings.

5. "Hate Crimes Against Hindus Continue to Rise, FBI Stats Show," Hindu American Foundation, December 30, 2019, www.hinduamerican.org/press/hate-crimes-against-hindus-continue-rise-fbi-stats-show.

Chapter Four: Anti-LGBTQ+ Hate Crimes

1. Cedeem Gumbs, "FX's Pose and the Importance of Representation in Media," *Refract Magazine*, www.refractmag.com/read/2019/11/26/fxs-pose-and-the-importance-of-representation-in-media (accessed November 10, 2020).

2. NCAVP, *Lesbian, Gay, Bisexual, Transgender, Queer, and HIV-Affected Hate Violence in 2016: A 20th Anniversary Report from the National Coalition of Anti-Violence Programs*, 2017.
3. Quoted in Gregory M. Herek, Jeanine C. Cogan, and J. Roy Gillis, "Victim Experiences in Hate Crimes Based on Sexual Orientation," *Journal of Social Issues*, 2002, vol. 58, p. 329.
4. Quoted in John M. Glionna, "Two Guilty of Killing Transgender Teen; the Men Bludgeoned and Choked Gwen Araujo After Accusing Her of Deceiving Them About Her Biological Identification," *Los Angeles Times*, September 13, 2005, p. B1.
5. J. G. Kosciw, C. M. Clark, N. L. Truong, and A.D Zongrone, *The 2019 National School Climate Survey: The Experiences of Lesbian, Gay, Bisexual, Transgender, and Queer Youth in Our Nation's Schools* (New York, NY: GLSEN, 2020).
6. Quoted in Bethany Barnes, "Gender Neutral Bathroom at Progressive Portland High School Tagged with Death Threat," *The Oregonian*, modified January 9, 2018, www.oregonlive.com/education/2017/03/gender_neutral_bathroom_at_pro.html.
7. KTVB Staff, "College of Idaho Pride Flags Vandalized in 'an Ugly Act of Hate'," KTVB, June 24, 2020, www.ktvb.com/article/news/local/208/college-of-idaho-pride-lgbtq-flags-vandalized-caldwell/277-7f1a4012-2223-4ee1-baeb-5082e40b939c.
8. Michaela Winberg, "After Surviving a Brutal Attack, Kendall Stephens Wants to Help Trans People Citywide," *Billy Penn*, Billy Penn, September 9, 2020, billypenn.com/2020/09/08/black-trans-woman-attack-philadelphia-kendall-stephens-survived-advocate-temple-student/.
9. Kevin Rector, "Hate Crime Investigation Underway after Transgender Women Robbed, Beaten in Hollywood," *Los Angeles Times*, August 19, 2020, www.latimes.com/california/story/2020-08-19/hate-crime-investigation-underway-after-transgender-women-robbed-beaten-in-hollywood.
10. "AMA Adopts New Policies on First Day of Voting at 2019 Annual Meeting," American Medical Association, June 10, 2019, www.ama-assn.org/press-center/press-releases/ama-adopts-new-policies-first-day-voting-2019-annual-meeting.

Chapter Five: Targeting Differences and Disabilities

1. Debra McKinney, "The Invisible Hate Crime," *Intelligence Report*, Southern Poverty Law Center, 2018 Fall Issue, *Confronting Hate*.
2. Laura Paterson, "New Campaign Launched Against Disability Hate Crimes," *The Scotsman*, March 4, 2020, www.scotsman.com/news/politics/new-campaign-launched-against-disability-hate-crimes-2072054.
3. Quoted in McKinney, "The Invisible Hate Crime."
4. Debra McKinney, "New York Woman Faces Hate Crime Charges for Targeting a Visually Impaired Man in a Burglary," *Southern Poverty Law Center*, July 20, 2018, www.splcenter.org/hatewatch/2018/07/20/new-york-woman-faces-hate-crime-charges-targeting-visually-impaired-man-burglary.
5. Brendan Campbell, et al. "Rising Hate Drives Latinos and Immigrants into Silence," Center for Public Integrity, August 22, 2018, publicintegrity.org/politics/rising-hate-drives-latinos-and-immigrants-into-silence/.
6. "Immigration Fervor Fuels Racist Extremism," Southern Poverty Law Center, 17 May 2006, www.splcenter.org/news/2006/05/17/immigration-fervor-fuels-racist-extremism.
7. "Immigration Fervor Fuels Racist Extremism."
8. Campbell, "Rising Hate Drives Latinos and Immigrants into Silence."

Chapter Six: Who Commits Hate Crimes?

1. Arno Michaelis, "This Is How You Become a White Supremacist," *The Washington Post*, March 1, 2019, www.washingtonpost.com/post everything/wp/2015/06/25/this-is-how-you-become-a-white-supremacist/.
2. "Frequently Asked Questions about Hate Groups," Southern Poverty Law Center, March 18, 2020, www.splcenter.org/20200318/frequently-asked-questions-about-hate-groups.
3. Sharon Jayson, "What Makes People Join Hate Groups?," *U.S. News & World Report*, August 23, 2017, www.usnews.com/news/national-news/articles/2017-08-23/what-makes-people-join-hate-groups-studies-say-childhood-torment-social-isolation.

4. John Eligon, "Racial Double Standard of Capitol Police Draws Outcry," *New York Times*, January 7, 2021, www.nytimes.com/2021/01/07/us/capitol-trump-mob-black-lives-matter.html.
5. Wesley Lowery, "More Whites Killed by Police, but Blacks 2.5 Times More Likely to Be Killed," *Chicago Tribune*, July 11, 2016, www.chicagotribune.com/news/nationworld/ct-police-shootings-race-20160711-story.html.
6. "Hate Violence Against Transgender Communities," National Coalition of Anti-Violence Programs, avp.org/wp-content/uploads/2017/04/ncavp_transhvfactsheet.pdf (accessed January 24, 2021).

Chapter Seven: Driving Out Darkness

1. Martin Luther King Jr., *Strength to Love* (New York, NY: Harper & Row, 1963), p. 53.
2. Associated Press, "Neo-Nazi Website Founder Owes $14 Million to Woman He Urged Readers to Harass, Judge Says," NBC News, August 9, 2019, www.nbcnews.com/news/us-news/neo-nazi-website-founder-owes-14-million-woman-he-urged-n1040671.
3. Daryl Davis, "What Do You Do When Someone Just Doesn't Like You?," TEDxCharlottesville, November 2017, Charlottesville, NC, www.ted.com/talks/daryl_davis_what_do_you_do_when_someone_just_doesn_t_like_you/transcript?language=en.
4. "About Teaching Tolerance," Teaching Tolerance, www.tolerance.org/about (accessed November 3, 2020).
5. Judy Shepard and Jon Barrett, *The Meaning of Matthew: My Son's Murder in Laramie, and a World Transformed* (New York, NY: Hudson Street Press, 2010), e-book.
6. Davis, "What Do You Do When Someone Just Doesn't Like You?"
7. Nelson Mandela, *Long Walk to Freedom* (New York, NY: MacDonald Purnell, 1994), e-book.

FOR MORE INFORMATION

Books: Nonfiction

Long, Michael G. *Kids on the March: 15 Stories of Speaking Out, Protesting, and Fighting for Justice*. Chapel Hill, NC: Algonquin Young Readers, 2021.

Lewis, John, Andrew Aydin, and Nate Powell. *March: Book One*. Marietta, GA: Top Shelf Productions, 2013.

McGraw, Sean Heather K. *The Gay Liberation Movement: Before and After Stonewall (History of the LGBTQ+ Rights Movement)*. New York, NY: Rosen Young Adult, 2019.

New York Times Educational Publishing. *Transgender Rights: Striving for Equality*. New York, NY: New York Times Educational Publishing in association with the Rosen Publishing Group, Inc., 2019.

Tyner, Artika, R. *Black Lives Matter: From Hashtag to the Streets*. Minneapolis, MN: Lerner Publications, 2021.

Books: Fiction

Thomas, Angie. *The Hate U Give*. New York, NY: Balzer + Bray, 2017.

Stone, Nic. *Dear Martin*. New York, NY: Crown Books for Young Readers, 2017.

Woodson, Jacqueline. *Harbor Me*. New York, NY: Nancy Paulsen Books, 2018.

Websites

11 Facts About Hate Crimes
www.dosomething.org/us/facts/11-facts-about-hate-crimes
Discover more facts about hate crimes on DoSomething.org, and get involved to do something about the problem of hate.

Federal Laws
stopbullying.gov/resources/laws/federal
Check out the Stop Bullying government website, which provides resources to youth experiencing violence. This page includes facts about federal laws for violence based on bias.

Hate Crimes
adl.org/what-we-do/combat-hate/hate-crimes
Learn how to combat hate crimes with the Anti-Defamation League (ADL). Read the latest research on hate crimes and how the ADL is working for justice for victims.

Hate Map
www.splcenter.org/hate-map
Check out this interactive hate map from the Southern Poverty Law Center, which shows where hate groups exist throughout the United States.

The Psychology of Hate Crimes
www.apa.org/advocacy/interpersonal-violence/hate-crimes
Learn more about the psychology behind hate crimes from the American Psychological Association.

Organizations

American Civil Liberties Union (ACLU)
125 Broad Street, 18th Floor
New York, NY 10004
www.aclu.org
www.instagram.com/aclu_nationwide/
twitter.com/aclu
www.youtube.com/aclu
The ACLU is a non-profit, non-partisan organization that fights on behalf of people who have had their civil liberties violated.

Anti-Defamation League (ADL)
605 Third Avenue
New York, NY 10158-3650
www.adl.org
www.instagram.com/adl_national/
twitter.com/ADL
www.youtube.com/user/ADLNational
The ADL fights hate crimes and discrimination across the world. Headquartered in the United States, the ADL provides education and resources for Americans about hate crimes.

Southern Poverty Law Center (SPLC)
400 Washington Avenue
Montgomery, AL 36104
www.instagram.com/splcenter/
www.splcenter.org
twitter.com/splcenter
The SPLC provides research, resources, and legal action in hate-crime cases.

The Trevor Project
PO Box 69232
West Hollywood, CA 90069
www.instagram.com/trevorproject/
www.thetrevorproject.org
thetrevorproject.tumblr.com/
twitter.com/trevorproject
www.youtube.com/thetrevorproject
The Trevor Project is a non-profit organization that focuses on mental health services for LGBTQ+ individuals.

Victim Connect Resource Center
(855) 484-2846
victimconnect.org
If you are the victim of a hate crime, you can use this website for help reporting a crime, learning about your rights, and developing self-care through difficult times. This resource center is a project of the National Center for Victims of Crime.

INDEX

A

alt-right, 28, 65–66
American-Arab Anti-Discrimination Committee, 83
American Civil War, 23, 65
American Guard, 69
American Medical Association (AMA), 52
Anti-Defamation League (ADL), 30, 37–38, 59, 83
Arc of the United States, 57

B

Bill of Rights, 35
Black Lives Matter, 18, 21–22, 69–74
Border Guardians, 58, 67
Brown, Michael, 70
Byrd, James, Jr., 24, 80

C

Catholics, 18, 35, 42–44, 65, 67
Chabad of Poway synagogue, 38–39
chimpanzees, 15
Christchurch, New Zealand, 41, 64
Christians, 14, 28, 35–38, 42–43, 64, 65
Confederate flag, 11, 29, 82
Constitution, 18, 23, 35
COVID-19 pandemic, 30, 60, 72

D

dehumanization, 17, 19, 37, 52
Don't Tolerate Hate campaign, 56

E

El Paso, Texas, 31, 60, 64

F

Federal Bureau of Investigation (FBI), 7, 18, 22, 26, 31, 35, 44–45, 49, 55, 58, 63, 69, 80–81
First Amendment, 18, 35
Floyd, George, 21, 70, 72
Frederick, Michael, Jr., 22, 32

G

Garner, Eric, 70, 74
genocide, 8
GLSEN, 50
Goodall, Jane, 15
Good Shepherd Church, 44
Griffith, Michael, 6

H

Hall, Candace, 22, 32
harassment, 19, 38, 49–51, 53, 56
Hate Crimes Against the Homeless Statistics Act, 60
Hate Crimes Prevention Act, 80
Hate Crime Statistics 2019, 22

Hate Crime Statistics Act, 7
hate music, 65, 69
Hindus, 35, 44–45
Hitler, Adolf, 36–37, 65
Holocaust, 5, 8, 36, 65
Human Rights Campaign (HRC), 52–53

I

Indian Citizenship Act, 27
Indigenous Women's Human Rights Collective, 28
Intelligence Project, 64
ISIS, 47
Islamophobia, 39

J

Jennings, Jazz, 48
Jewish people, 5, 8, 35–39, 42, 64–65, 67, 83, 85

K

King, Rodney, 74
Ku Klux Klan (KKK), 18, 23, 28, 37, 65, 83–84

L

Life After Hate, 84
lynching, 23, 31, 65

M

Marshall Project, 7
Martin, Trayvon, 21
media, 48, 68, 76
Mexican Cession, 31
Michaelis, Arno, 63–64, 84
Muslims, 14, 18, 35–36, 28–44, 64–65, 67

N

National Alliance to End Homelessness, 60
National Association for the Advancement of Colored People (NAACP), 26, 72, 83
National Coalition of Anti-Violence Programs (NCAVP), 49
National Coalition for the Homeless (NCH), 60–61
National Inmate Survey, 76
National School Climate Survey, 50
National Socialist Movement (NSM), 65, 67
Nazis, 5, 8, 36–37, 64–65, 67–69, 83
Not In Our Town (NIOT), 85–86

O

Obama, Barack, 80

P

Pew Research Center, 59–60
Proud Boys, 69
Pulse nightclub, 47

Q

al-Qaeda, 40, 42
Queen of Peace Catholic Church, 44

R

Rice, Tamir, 70

Roof, Dylann, 11–12, 41

S

September 11 attacks, 39
Shepard, Matthew, 17, 51, 80
Sikhs, 35, 42–43, 45
social media, 18, 41, 60, 64, 68–69, 86
Southern Poverty Law Center (SPLC), 7–8, 18, 28, 55–56, 64, 83, 86
stereotypes, 13–14, 16–17, 30, 32, 42, 68
Stonewall Riots, 49
Stormfront White Nationalist Community, 69

T

Taylor, Breonna, 72
Tell MAMA (Measuring Anti-Muslim Attacks), 41
Texas Minutemen, 67
13th Amendment, 23
Tree of Life synagogue, 7
Trevor Project, 53
Trump, Donald, 7, 18, 28–29, 31, 40, 51, 57, 66
Tulsa Race Massacre, 24–25

U

"Unite the Right" rally, 28, 65, 68
University College London, 14
U.S. Department of Justice, 6

V

Vietnam War, 29

W

Westboro Baptist Church (WBC), 67
white nationalist groups, 28–29, 41, 64–66, 69
white supremacy, 7, 11, 18, 21–23, 25, 28, 31–32, 41, 63, 66, 69, 72, 79, 84–85
Williamson, Mercedes, 80
World War II, 8, 37

X

xenophobia, 18, 30, 57

PHOTO CREDITS

Cover Christopher Penler/Shutterstock.com; p. 4 DAVE LINTOTT/Contributor/AFP/Getty Images; pp. 10, 88 Anadolu Agency/Contributor/Anadolu Agency/Getty Images; p. 14 vector_s/iStock/Getty Images Plus/Getty Images; p. 17 Daisy-Daisy/iStock/Getty Images Plus/Getty Images; p. 19 Steve Liss/Contributor/The LIFE Images Collection/Getty Images; p. 20 Samuel Corum/Stringer/Getty Images News/Getty Images; p. 25 Everett Collection/Shutterstock.com; p. 26 skynesher/E+/Getty Images; pp. 29, 62 NurPhoto/Contributor/NurPhoto/Getty Images; p. 30 Boston Globe/Contributor/Boston Globe/Getty Images; pp. 32, 60 Mario Tama/Staff/Getty Images News/Getty Images; p. 34 Spencer Platt/Staff/Getty Images News/Getty Images; p. 38 SOPA Images/Contributor/LightRocket/Getty Images; p. 40 JIM WATSON/Staff/AFP/Getty Images; p. 41 Scott Barbour/Stringer/Getty Images News/Getty Images; p. 43 ajaykampani/E+/Getty Images; p. 44 Hank Walker/Contributor/The LIFE Picture Collection/Getty Images; p. 45 The Washington Post/Contributor/The Washington Post/Getty Images; p. 46 Roy Rochlin/Stringer/Getty Images Entertainment/Getty Images; p. 48 Scott Olson/Staff/Getty Images News/Getty Images; p. 52 Andrew Francis Wallace/Contributor/Toronto Star/Getty Images; p. 54 SeventyFour/iStock/Getty Images Plus/Getty Images; p. 58 a katz/Shutterstock.com; p. 65 Eric-Paul-Pierre PASQUIER/Contributor/Gamma-Rapho/Getty Images; p. 67 David S. Holloway/Contributor/Getty Images News/Getty Images; p. 68 (top) Douglas Graham/Contributor/CQ-Roll Call, Inc./Getty Images; p. 68 (bottom) Sisoje/E+/Getty Images; p. 69 Steven D Starr/Contributor/Corbis Historical/Getty Images; p. 73 Ira L. Black - Corbis/Contributor/Corbis News/Getty Images; p. 75 Pool/Pool/Getty Images News/Getty Images; p. 76 Zolnierek/iStock/Getty Images Plus/Getty Images; p. 78 Kevin Dodge/The Image Bank/Getty Images; p. 81 Fourleaflover/iStock/Getty Images Plus/Getty Images; p. 82 FatCamera/E+/Getty Images; p. 85 Chuck Nacke/Alamy Stock Photo; p. 87 Star Tribune via Getty Images/Contributor/Star Tribune/Getty Images.

ABOUT THE AUTHOR

C.R. McKay is a children's author and editor from Buffalo, NY. She has written more than 600 books for young people, including educational nonfiction, graphic novels, and fiction. She believes in the power of loving kindness, education, and respectful dialogue to change the world.